I0832507

LIFE-BOATS,

PROJECTILES,

AND OTHER MEANS FOR

SAVING LIFE;

BY

R. B. FORBES.

BOSTON:
WM. PARSONS LUNT,
102 WASHINGTON STREET,
1872.

JAMES F. COTTER & CO., PRINTERS,
14 State Street,
BOSTON.

INTRODUCTION.

It will be seen on reading the following pages, that there is very little if any original matter contained therein.

It is to be hoped however that the renewal of many old suggestions made by the writer, and others, may be productive of good, and be the means of calling the attention of those who manufacture laws, to the growing necessity for increased care in protecting the lives of those who go to sea.

Whatever may be the award of the public in regard to this little work as a literary composition, the writer will rest content with having tried to mitigate the dangers of the sea, and will consider his time and money well spent, if through these means a single life shall be saved.

LIFE-BOATS.

In discussing the qualities considered necessary in a life-boat, the Committee appointed to award the premium of one hundred guineas offered by the Duke of Northumberland, in 1851, rank the qualities necessary for a good life-boat as hereunder:

Qualities for Rowing in all weathers, ...	20
Sailing in all weathers, ...	18
As a sea boat, as to stability, safety, bouyancy at bow for launching, ...	10
Small internal capacity for water up to the level of the thwarts, ...	9
Means of freeing easily of water, ...	8
Extra buoyancy; its nature, amount, distribution, and mode of application, ...	7
Power of self-righting, ...	6
Suitableness for beaching, ...	4
Room for passengers, ...	3
Protection from injury to bottom, ...	3
Ballast; iron, 1, water, 2, cork, 3, ...	6
Access to stem or stern, ...	3
Timber heads for warps, ...	2
Fenders, life-lines, etc., ...	1
	100

This is, no doubt, a very fair estimate of the qualities considered necessary for boats for the coasts of Great Britain, where many of them are located in harbors of refuge, under pier heads or breakwaters, where they can have the aid of steam tugs to get them to the scene of disaster, and also the aid of the men of the coast guard assisted by a dense population.

Of thirty boats offered for competition described in the report alluded to and selected as coming near to the standard of excellence out of two hundred and eighty, the one to which the award was given was built by James Beeching, of Great Yarmouth; length, 36 feet over all, 31 feet keel, beam, 9½ feet, depth, 3½ feet amidships, with 3 feet sheer; amount of extra buoyancy in air, 300 cubic feet, or 8½ tons: internal capacity for water up to the thwarts, 5 tons; area of delivering tubes, 276 square inches; proportion of delivery area to capacity, 1 to 64; weight, 7,504 lbs.; ballast, 2 tons water, ½-ton iron keel; draught of water with 30 men on board, 2 feet 2 inches; oars, 12 double banked; rig, 2 lugs; cost, £250; outside a cork fender 6 inches wide by 8 inches deep, 7 inches below gunwale. The extra buoyancy is in air cases in the bottom and on part of the sides and in the ends for a length of 8½ feet to the height of the gunwale. The water ballast there is a tank with compartments in the bottom amidships, 14 feet long by 5 wide, and 15 inches high, containing 77 cubic feet, equal to 2 tons, and an iron keel of 10 cwt. The delivery valves are 8, of 6 inches diameter, 4, of 4 inches; weight, 50 cwt., and gear 17 cwt., total, 3 tons 7 cwt. Can carry 70 persons; keel, 8 inches.

The Committee awarding to this boat a premium of one hundred guineas, remark as to her qualities:

"The form is good for pulling and sailing in all weathers; in places like Yarmouth, where there are plenty of hands to launch her, the weight would cause no difficulty. By means of the large raised air-cases in the ends; the abscence of air-cases for a length of 10 feet amidships; the introduction of 2 tons of water into her bottom, and the iron keel of half a ton, she would right herself when capsized, although, from her form, it would be difficult to capsize her. A passage or gap should be left in the large end of the tanks to admit of men approaching the ends. The deep keel, though favorable for sailing and for assisting to right her, will be objectionable in landing on a beach, and would render her more difficult to turn in the event of desiring to put her end on to a heavy roller. The area of delivery valves is large enough to free her rapidly, so that with her crew on board only a few inches of water would remain on the floor. The air-cases being built into the boat, and a part of the shell, renders them liable to accidents; if this were remedied, and her internal capacity reduced, a 30 or 32 foot boat on similar model, with internal fittings slightly modified, would make an efficient life-boat, adapted for many parts of our coast."

Remarks on the Beeching Boat:

Without undertaking to insist upon the acceptance of my views as entirely orthodox, and yet believing that the experience I have gained by long study and practice entitles them to consideration, I shall review the descriptions given and give my opinion for what it is worth.

In the Journal of the Royal Institution for April, 1872, there is a plan of the boat now most approved, which is 33 feet long, 8 feet beam, wherein the water-ballast seems to have given place to cork in separate compartments. This boat is said to combine the following qualities: great stability, speed, facility for launching and landing, immediate self-freeing of water, self-righting, strength, and stowage for a large number of extra persons. The principal objections to this premium boat for use on our coast are the weight and cost, and the steering by a rudder; also, the deep keel would be very objectionable for landing and quick turning to meet a roller. The air-cases should be detachable.

The recommendation of the Committee as to reduced size and some change in the internal fittings, seems to have been carried out in the boat above alluded to, as adopted by the Royal Institution.

Another boat, by Geo. Palmer, which may be considered as near the extreme on the side of lightness, is thus described:

Length, 26 feet; beam, 6¾; depth, 3¼; sheer, 20 inches; keel, 3; extra buoyancy; air, 82 cubic feet, equal to 2½ tons; internal capacity up to the level of thwarts, 1¾ tons; area of delivery valves, none; weight, 15 cwt.; ballast, none; draught with 22 men in her, 15 inches; 5 oars, single bank; no sails; cost £75. Form general like a whaleboat; has a cork fender, 4 inches diameter, along the sides near the gunwale. The extra buoyancy is obtained by detached air-cases of wood, 18 inches square, along the sides up to the level of the thwarts, and in the bow and stern sheets up to the gunwale, divided into 12 compartments, and by the fenders; no means of freeing of water except by bailing; weight of the shell, 10 cwt., and of gear, 5 cwt.

Remarks of the Committee:

"This boat would pull well, be light for transportation, easily manned, has small internal capacity for holding water, all good points in her favor; but she would not be self-righting, the air-cases in the ends would prevent a near approach to the ends, she is narrow for her length, and her rising floor would be unfavorable for landing. This model has generally been adopted by the Royal National Institution, and is said to have saved many lives."

The principal objections to the form and fittings of this boat are the rise of floor, as noted by the Committee, would make her unfit for landing on a beach. The steering by a rudder, as represented in the plan, is very objectionable. She would not be self-righting: on the other hand, she would in the event of capsizing, be easily righted, and it would not be difficult speedily to bail her out; she could not be swamped; is light to carry along shore; and not costly; with a steering oar, and less dead rise amidships, she wonld be much better for our coast than the heavy Beeching boat.

Another by Lord John Hay, is described thus:

Length 32⅔; beam, 7½; depth, including keel, 3.10; sheer, 26; extra buoyancy, air 200 cubic feet, equal to 6 tons; internal capacity up to thwarts, 4 tons; area of valves, 240 square inches; proportion, 1 to 6; weight, 32 cwt.; ballast, none; draught, with 30 men, 18 inches; oars, 14; cost, £70.

Remarks by Committee:

"Form like a whaleboat, long flat floor, built of narrow strakes pinned together through the edges, (supposed double planked,) without timbers, of mahogany, and copper-fastened; 7 thwarts 25 inches apart, 9 below the gunwale, 11 above the floor; pulls 14 oars, double-banked. The extra buoyancy is obtained by an air-case under the floor, 20 inches deep; air-cases in the ends for 6½ feet, up to gunwale. These cases divided into compartments and detached from the shell, so as to be removable at will; no ballast. The means for freeing her of water consists in five scuppers on each side, 5 by 4 inches, on a level with the flooring, the area of which is 240 square inches. The water is led to the scuppers by a shoot or water-course under the thwarts, raised 4 inches above the floor with the entrance amidships, so that in rolling the water will not come into the boat through the scuppers. The provision for righting consists in the raised ends; no sails; steered by a sweep at either end. She can carry 60 persons."

Remarks by the Committee:

"This boat will pull well in smooth water, but her light draft and large surface in a strong wind and sea would retard her. She would sail fast going free, is light for her length and easily transported, has small internal capacity for water, (in fact none.) In experiments *with the model*, it was found that the entrance of the scuppers amidships delayed the exit of the water. An advantage of the side outlets over the usual valves through the bottom is that they would be less liable to be choaked in grounding. The provision for righting, namely, good sheer and raised end cases, fully answered the purpose; mode of construction, good; detached air-cases very good and the cork covering for their protection might be generally adopted; a passage to within two feet of the stem desirable; extra buoyancy ample in amount, but its disposition questionable; as a general rule, extra buoyancy should be placed high up; in this model 200 square feet of buoyancy are in the bottom, under the floor, which lies 24 inches above the bottom of the keel, or 5 inches above the water line, with 30 men in her, without any compensating ballast. The centre of gravity would thus be so high as to endanger stability, and were a sea to break into her, she would capsize; were this point remedied by substituting cork for some of the air cases in the bottom, she would be a serviceable boat in a rapid tide-way."

By substituting cork for half of the air and making a different arrangement to deliver the water coming over the floor, and fitting the oars to run with grommets, spreading the thwarts so as to give more room for the steersman and for 12 double bank oars instead of 14, and reduce the keel near the ends to nothing, this boat would be well adapted to our coast, though long for her beam; the detachable cases is an excellent feature to be commended for all life-boats.

Another boat, by Henry Hinks, Appledore, is 30 feet long, 9 beam, 3 deep, 2 sheer, extra buoyancy, cork and air 105 cubic feet equal to 3 tons, internal capacity up to thwarts 3⅓ tons, area of delivery 72 square inches, proportion of delivery to capacity 1 to 1.6, weight 35 cwt., ballast none, draught with 30 men, 18, 12 oars double banked, cost £110. The body like a cutter, ends like a whaleboat, flat long floor, built of mahogany and copper fastened, keel 5 inches and bilge pieces, cork fender 5x5 outside, 12 inches below the rail or gunwale and near to upper side of air cases, bottom sheathed with cork 3 inches thick to water line. The extra buoyancy is obtained by air cases in bilge and side carried on a slope rounding towards amidships to the top of the floor or grating, laid 9 inches above the keelson, average width of the cases 18 inches by 12 deep, and air-cases 4 feet long in the ends, the whole comprising 16 compartments, built into the boat, and to be lined with copper or gutta percha and by the cork fenders; no ballast. Provision for righting consists in the end cases; no rig; steered by a sweep at either end, will carry 40 persons.

Remarks of the Committee:

"Form good for pulling in all weathers and would sail well free; light for transportation and heavy enough to maintain momentum; small internal capacity and might be reduced to advantage; area of delivery might be larger, but the gunwale strake about 10 inches deep between end tanks, being left out and the slope of the fore-and-aft cases running to the floor, much of the water shipped would roll out through the open upper strake. The provision for righting consists in the end cases, and the absence of any flat side cases which would enable her to right easily. An iron keel of 5 cwt. would insure this—all the cases are formed in the boat and liable to be stove, it would be better to have all detachable, a passage should be left in the end cases for approach to the ends of boat; with attention to these details she would be a suitable life-boat for many parts of the coast."

I consider the general proportions of this boat with the exception of the rake of the ends, which ought to be greater, and the straight keel, as better for our coast than either of the preceding ones, the keel should be reduced to 2 inches in centre and rounded off to nothing, and give her a centre-board of iron which would make her weatherly under sail and add a trifle to her stability, the opening at the sides from the end tanks, about

10 inches deep is a very good feature, the depth of the closed part being sufficient for a boat of her size say 21 inches amidships from the top of keel or garboard, this would enable her to right with a little help, the only objection I see to the opening is the liability to stave the gunwale where the tholes and grommets ship by making this very strong there would be little danger of rupture while the fender remains intact.

Another by Farrow of South Shields, 30 long, 10 beam, 3.9 deep, sheer 2½, buoyancy extra 200 cubic feet or 6 tons, internal capacity for water 3½ tons, area of delivery 96 square inches, proportion to capacity 1 to 1¼, weight 57 cwt., iron keel 5 cwt., 65 cwt., water 3 tons, draught with 30 men on board 30 inches, 10 oars double bank, no rig, cost £130.

"Form similar to paddle-box boat, flat floor, raking stem and stern, full end-lines, 20 inches camber or round of keel, cork fender outside, 1 foot wide, 9 inches below gunwale, the extra buoyancy is obtained by an air case, 15 inches deep, fore and aft above the well, and 30 in the ends, by side air-cases sloping from gunwale to the floor, and end cases 6 feet long, the whole divided into compartments and built into the boat, extra buoyancy, air 6 tons, cork 2, ballast in a tank 14 feet long, by 15 inches, extending from side to side of bottom, divided by transverse partitions to prevent the washing of water, with limber holes, the tank may be closed when full and is provided with air tubes, and she has an iron keel, means of delivery are by 10 tubes of 3½ inches diameter; provision for righting consists in the water ballast, iron keel, and end cases; no rig; steers with a sweep."

Remarks of the Committee:

"Will pull well in smooth water, sail fast free, be buoyant and lively, be turned rapidly, but would not steer steadily; small internal capacity for water, up to thwarts; fair amount of delivery, but will bear increasing; ample extra buoyancy, chiefly attained in the air-case under the floor: if, under any circumstances this is desirable, it is compensated here by the large amount of ballast; but the difficulty of keeping the bulkheads tight, and the danger of the water finding its way into the head or stern, induces the Committee to prefer cork in the bottom, which acts as ballast and buoyancy also in case of emergency. Farrow claims to be the inventor of water-tank ballast, dating back to 1843. The system is now common. Provision for righting consists in good sheer, end air-cases, water and iron ballast, and is ample; a good passage is left free to the ends and room for sweep steering oar. She is a fair type of the Tyne and Wear life-boats. The builder gained the prize at South Shields, Dec. 1841, and at Newcastle, March, 1850."

This boat has plenty of beam and rake of ends, as well as round of keel, in fact is an exaggeration of what I recommend in the last, and the ends are described as very full, like the nearly obsolete paddle-box boat. She would be too heavy for our coast,—5,600 lbs. The Committee say she would turn rapidly by her steering oar, which is a vitally important feature for a surf-boat. They also say she would not steer steadily; from which I dissent, for if she can be turned easily that is a quality which if used aright will surely enable her to be steered straight; a boat with a long keel of 4 or 5 inches deep, being hard to turn by the steering oar, is also hard to get straight when slewed by the sea or the griping under a press of sail. This boat is too rounding, and I should say that a boat with less would be a happy medium, so far as handling is concerned, between this boat and one with a perfectly straight keel. Less water ballast and more cork would improve her. I cannot appreciate the alleged difficulty of keeping the bulkheads in tank tight enough to prevent undue oscillation of the water ballast.

Boat by White, of Cowes:

"32 long, 8 beam, 3 deep, sheer, 1½; extra buoyancy 75 cubic feet, or 2 tons; water capacity to thwarts, 3 tons; no delivery valves; draft 12 inches; 6 oars, single bank; weight 30 cwt.; 1 lug sail; cost, £75. Form of whaleboat, slightly rising floor amidships, moderate rake of ends, carvel built and copper fastened; keel 4 inches, straight; extra buoyancy is obtained by air-cases round the sides internally sloping from gunwale to floor, and end cases 5 feet long, divided into compartments and built into the boat; no delivery valves; provision for righting consists in the end tanks; rig, 1 lug; steers by a rudder; draught with 30 men in her, 21 inches; will carry 30 persons."

Remarks by Committee :

"Form good for pulling and sailing in all weathers; a good sea boat; light for transportation; has much less extra buoyancy than usual in life-boats, but is ample for common purposes, but the air-cases being built into the boat is objectionable; the internal capacity for water is not large, but she has no delivery valves—no means of freeing herself of water save by rolling it out, which would be facilitated by the shape of the inside air-cases; not likely to upset, but if upset, the small sheer, with no ballast in water or keel, would not enable her to right herself; has less beam than usual, but might be well adapted to a rapid tide-way."

This boat wants more beam and more rake of ends, reduction of keel to two inches outside of garboard, tapering off to nothing at the scarf; a long steering oar fitted to be used at either end, in place of the rudder, as shown in the plan, and a centre-board. She is called light for an English boat, say 3,360 lbs., but would be considered too heavy here. Air-cases undetachable are always objectionable; to have them movable would increase weight and cost. This boat would not capsize easily, but ought to be righted and bailed out without much effort.

Boat by Lieut. B. Sharpe, R. N.:

"30 long over all, 23 keel, 8 beam, 3½ deep, 2 sheer; extra buoyancy 320 square feet cork, equal to 6¾ tons; no room for water, consequently no delivery valves; weight, 25 cwt.; iron keel, 3 cwt.; draught with 30 men, 2 feet; 10 double bank and two single oars; 1 lug sail; cost, £70.

"Form of whaleboat, with less beam, long flat floor, very raking ends, fender of cork outside; extra buoyancy, cork only in bundles up to the thwarts, connected by rope, so as to be removed and made into a raft; room made for crew and passengers by removal of bundles; a canvas cover over all the cork; a cone of cork at each end, 5 feet long by 2½ at base and rising above gunwale 6 inches: effective extra buoyancy equal to 4 tons; ballast, a short flat iron keel 1½ cwt.; no internal capacity for water, (except where legs go,) any water coming in above the cover is to leave by an opening 5 feet long in the upper strake on each side, opening outwards on hinges; provision for righting consists in the end cones, the iron keel, and 2 sliding keels to be used when necessary ; no sail ; steers with a sweep at either end ; will carry 20 persons ; *beam, 5 feet ; cost, £35.

Remarks of Committee, on the description, and not on the plans.

"Form to pull fast in smooth water, but in a sea way and breeze would be difficult to steer, light for transporting and easy to launch, the raised cones and keel would enable her to right easily and her short keel would enable her to turn quickly. The characteristic feature of this boat is the filling inside up to the thwarts with cork whereby there is little space for water and great buoyancy acting also as ballast.

"If sufficient buoyancy can be got by cork, and there is no evidence to the contrary, it is far preferable to air-cases, the best mode of distribution requires consideration; in this case (the narrow boat) too much is sacrificed to the desire to form a raft, which does not appear of sufficient advantage to lose the space required for passengers and inconvenience to the rowers, the raised cones are objectionable as they interfere with access to the ends, one important advantage of this plan is that it is not liable to injury like air cases, and it can be easily applied to a common boat and much benefit would arise from thus fitting fishing boats, coast guard boats and any others subject to exposure to sudden gales and casualties."

I highly approve of the general form of this boat, flat floor, good sheer, some round of keel, fine ends, and rake enough to enable her to slew easily by the steering oar, this applies to the plan and not to the description above given, the plan gives beam 8 feet while the description gives only 5, the principal objection I see to the plan is a want of standing-room for the proper handling of the steering oar; in order to give this room which is vital to a surf-boat, one thwart must be removed, the plan shows 7 thwarts, and the intention is to pull on five of them 10 double bank short oars, and near the tapering ends on the other thwarts a somewhat longer single oar, making 12 oars, it will be better to have only the 10 short double banked oars, or 8

---

*This description is different in beam and otherwise to the plan from which the dimensions are taken.

double bank and two single, ten men is crew enough for a boat of 30 feet, the plan shows an open strake between the end tanks for a distance of 20 feet, so that she may be properly described as a solid cork buoy with spaces for the legs of the crew, the sliding keels alluded to are not distinctly illustrated in the plan and probably don't amonnt to much.

The idea of connecting the bundles of cork together by ropes, so as to avail of them for making a raft does not appear to me to be practical; in the event of danger to a sinking vessel, if there were no other means for constructing a raft, this cork might come in play, but taking it out from under the thwarts of this boat under such circumstances would render the boat herself quite useless and it would obviously be better to keep the boat intact or remove only a part of the cork to make room for more legs, and have cork or air rafts to save part of the people. Notwithstanding the obvious defects in the plan as above stated, I cannot but think the general plan of nearly filling the boat with cork can be made practically useful in deciding on a suitable life-boat for our coasts as well as for steamers. The boat in question is said to weigh 2,800 pounds, too much for us, though very light for an English life-boat; I dissent entirely from the idea of fitting fishing-boats in this manner, they require all the room they can get for nets, fish, etc.

Boat by Joseph Francis, New York.—No plan given; described as hereunder.

"27 long, extreme; length of flat 22, beam 7, 2½ deep, sheer 27 inches, rake 7 inches to the foot, built of corrugated galvanized iron, 6 thwarts, 15 inches wide, 21 apart, 6 below gunwale, and 20 above the floor; air-cases under them dividing the boat into six separate compartments, each having a delivery plug 3 inches in diameter on the side for the escape of water. A stout rope fender with life-lines attached to it is carried round the boat, 9 inches below the gunwale, extra buoyancy is obtained by cone shaped air-cases, 4½ feet long, which at their square ends rise 20 inches above the gunwale, and by air-cases under the thwarts, effective buoyancy 75 square feet, or 2 tons, no ballast, internal capacity for water up to thwarts 110 cubic feet, or 3 tons, nothing in the model to show means of freeing herself; provision for righting by the air-cases at the ends, no sails, said to carry 20 persons, 6 single bank oars, and a sweep steering oar, draught with crew 20 inches, weight of boat 9 cwt., and of gear 4 cwt., cost £45."

The metallic car is thus described: "a shallow flat boat of galvanized iron, ends alike, 26 feet long, 7 beam, 3½ deep, straight stern and keel; it has a high cone shaped cover rising from each end to 4½ feet above the gunwale amidships, where a space of six feet is left for the main hatchway; otherwise every other part is tight, the object being, after communication is established, to put passengers in and drag them ashore through the surf unharmed, the testimonial accompanying the model states that in the wreck of the Ayrshire on the coast of New Jersey, January 12, 1850, 201 men, women and children, and infants were landed in safety by one of these cars by the United States Government, who in 1849 established 8 life-boat stations 10 miles apart between Sandy Hook and Little Egg Harbor, the stations are furnished with boats, cars, rockets and mortars, at a cost of £2,000."

Remarks of the Committee:

"The corrugated galvanized iron said to combine lightness, strength, economy and durability; the light weight, if no more than stated renders transportation easy, and her strength would enable her to land on a rocky beach unharmed, the end case and the absence of side cases might cause her to right. As a surf-boat, if by that term is meant merely for landing on a beach, the shallow form might be suitable, but it is not adaptable to the general purposes of a life-boat as used in this country to go off shore to a stranded vessel. The high end cases and flat bottom would render her difficult to pull against wind and sea and hard to steer. Water shipped might perhaps be rolled out, otherwise there is no provision for freeing herself and with the crew on board it would be within 4 inches of the thwarts. The end cases prevent approach to the ends, a serious objection in approaching a wreck end on. The printed testimonials are much in favor of the metal boats, which are stationed on the coast by the Government, but with respect to the life surf-boat there is a want of sufficient evidence as to the nature of the shore, the distance the boat had to go, the state of the weather, and of the sea, all of which are important points in considering the subject; sufficient however is adduced to establish that in strength, lightness, durability and economy, metal boats have great advantages for particular purposes."

"Since the above was written a full sized boat similar to the model has arrived; on weighing her she was found to weigh 19 cwt. instead of 9; on trial, in smooth water, it was found that with plugs out and 6 men in her, the water stood level with the thwarts, and on adding 5 cwt. of ballast, the water rose to within 3 inches of the gunwale, the boat turned over throwing her crew into the water and she lay still bottom up, and on the men taking hold of her to right her she turned over twice like a cask; thus proving that however fit she may be for a surf-boat, on the coast of America she is quite unsuitable, in her present form, for the general purpose of a life-boat on any part of the coast of this country."

The description given of this boat differs considerably from any I remember to have seen, and I may say the same of the car, 26 feet long, 7 beam, etc., therefore I shall confine my remarks mainly to the things described; if the testimonial accompanying the model of the life-car illustrating its actual use in the case of the Ayrshire in 1849, gives the idea that the fortunate car was like the description given by the committee, I can only say that it differs very much from the car illustrated in Francis blue-book, as well as from those belonging to the Humane Society of Massachusetts, bought of the Francis Life-boat Co., and said to be similar to the one which rescued the Ayrshire's people. The opening remarks of the Committee go for little when we come to read the postscript, wherein the weight of a full-sized boat was found to be 19 cwt. and not 9 cwt., arising probably from a typographical error.

The trial in smooth water fully confirms the unfavorable opinion I have formed of the Francis Boat. It has long been the opinion of our surf men that the metallic boats placed by the Government on the coast of New Jersey, and those given to the Massachusetts Humane Society by the same, are practically valueless as surf-boats. The Humane Society were very glad to receive and house these boats at the time, thinking there might be cases where ships with emigrants might find them useful. The Society have six situated at the following points; Nantucket Bar, Monomoy, Chatham, Nausett, Gloucester, Scituate, they were handed over to the Society by the Secretary of the Treasury, June 5, 1855, since that time, so far as I remember, their record of services stands thus: Nantucket once manned in a comparatively smooth time, and found to pull well; Monomoy boat was made use of to take the crew off a vessel about 15 years ago, and having no very rough water did the work well; Chatham boat has never been distinguished in saving life; Nausett has been afloat two or three times, once in very cold weather within a year or two, but the wind was off shore, the sea not rough, the seamen say that they would not have attempted to go off in her had it been rough; the Scituate boat has never been utilized in saving life; the Gloucester boat has been made useful on several occasions in boarding wrecks in comparatively smooth water, pulling out of the harbor, but has never been subjected to a severe trial.

There can be no doubt as to the strength and durability under all changes of climate of the corrugated iron boat; those we received of the Government in 1855, are perfectly good now and have required only painting; by fitting them with detachable end cases, large cork fenders, and air-cases inside sufficient to keep the water, with large valves open and crew on board, down to five inches below the thwarts, they can be made very useful for ship's boats and for steamers.

The Raymond Boat, also made of galvanized iron, not corrugated, and fitted with detachable end tanks and air cases under the thwarts at the sides, is a very useful, strong, durable ship's boat, but I have never seen a Francis or a Raymond Boat that can be said to fulfil the conditions of self-righting, and self-freeing of water, which are essential in a true life-boat.

The object in giving these details and expressing these views, is to show to general readers interested in the subject what kind of boats are most approved in Great Britain, and to have the benefit of the experience of experts in that line. In the above list, comprising only seven of the thirty most approved out of two hundred and eighty plans and models, a sufficient variety is given to illustrate the subject and to prepare the way for a discussion of their merits, and thus endeavor to inaugurate a system which shall be applicable to our coasts in the vicinity of our principal ports, and also to our passenger vessels.

The question as to the best vehicle is not easily answered. The question as to what will be the best surf-boat for the open beaches of New Jersey, Long Island, Nantucket, Cape Cod, Cape Ann, etc., is still undecided, and after all my experience I cannot recommend any well known and well recognized system as appropriate to all these and other localities on the great lakes. Seamen brought up on the coast have their own ideas as to the kind of vehicle they require when they are to risk their lives to save life and property. Their wishes and their prejudices must, to a certain extent, be consulted. If, on the coast of New Jersey, they prefer the model which experience has taught them to reverence; with a flat bottom, broad stern, sloping sides and considerable sheer, built of cedar or light corrugated iron, let them have such, but we must insist on it that no man shall go afloat, rough or smooth, without a cork life-belt, made after the English style, but slightly less buoyant and expensive, and every boat should be furnished with enough spare ones contained in boxes under the thwarts to supply her full carrying capacity. She should have detachable end tanks, and outside solid cork fenders fastened half-way between the gunwale and the load-line; they should be large enough to give stability when the boat ships water; they will then be very valuable, though they will make it more difficult to right her when capsized; this we cannot help. It is a very difficult question to decide as to the just medium between too much weight and too little buoyancy when she ships water. A boat built of light wood, 30x8 and 3 deep, need not weigh over 1,000 lbs., and the chances are that a boat of this weight can be got off and on through a surf, the men being supplied with life-belts, when no boat called a life-boat and deserving the name could be manned and got off *on the Jersey coast by Jersey beach men.*

I presume the same remarks apply to the coast of Long Island.

At Nantucket, where the surf is heavy and the beaches frequently steep, the surf-men prefer light wooden clincher-built boats, with large beam and considerable sheer, pulling long oars, single bank, and steering like whaleboats. By attaching vulcanized rubber cylinders outside, or stout cork fenders, with end air-cases, these boats will stand up with considerable water and a large crew in them, and in case of being stoven, they can be got on shore with some risk and difficulty; but the rubber cylinders are constantly giving trouble by imperfections in the valves and bellows, and the air-cannisters, unless made of heavy copper, deteriorate very fast and offer a prize to the rascals who infest our coasts and steal our ropes, oars, etc.; for these reasons I have concluded to depend mostly on cork for extra buoyancy, and to limit this, so that a boat shall not weigh over 1,500 lbs. with all her fittings.

Leaving Nantucket, we come to the Cape shore. In the vicinity of Chatham and Orleans, the surf-men use for their fishing and wrecking purposes, full built, flat round bottomed cedar built boats, both ends alike, and they naturally feel confidence in them, and will risk their lives in them when nothing would induce them to attempt to launch a life-boat weighing a ton only.

Going a little further to Provincetown we find that they want boats more like whaleboats but with more beam, fair sheer and very much shoaler than the Orleans boats, very light built, boats that pull 5 oars, and that can be picked up bodily by five or six men, and run off to meet the rollers, it requires considerable urging to induce them to admit any extra buoyancy, or even to put on their belts. Now we cross over to Cape Ann, here the seamen have nearly all been long accustomed to handling dories pulling short oars cross handed, the largest pulling 4 and the rest 2 oars, a well managed dory will get off of a rough beach dry, when no other boat can, and are very useful at times in saving life by carrying off a line, etc., but they are worthless for landing numbers of clumsy passengers. Brought up to the short oar the Cape Ann and Marblehead men want double bank boats, therefore, as a general rule it is desirable to consult the people whom we are to call upon in time of need.

Taking into view the prejudices and preferences of our coast men, giving due weight to their wishes, if I had the means and authority to inaugurate a system of boats, including durability, economy in the long run, and ability to command the confidence of the men who are to use them, I think I should build light corrugated iron boats about 25 feet, 6½ beam, and 30 inches deep, with good sheer say 15 inches, flat midship section and not very fine ends with centre-boards, to pull at Nantucket, 5 oars single bank, elsewhere I should fit them to pull 6 short oars double bank and one at the bow thwart single, the standing room should not be less in length than that of a whaleboat, say from the sternpost becket to the after thwart about 8 feet, much depends on the steering oar and it is most important to have plenty of room to operate it successfully; on the outside I should lash securely, cork fenders, made of solid pieces with a rope rove through the centre and cover them with the best cotton canvas, well sewed so as to exclude the water as long as possible; these should be placed far enough below the gunwale to clear the oars, but not far enough to drag in the water: say 6 inches below the gunwale amidships; in the ends, an air cannister of copper, or cork fastened together in a mass, sufficient to *assist* in righting her—more we cannot expect of them with the opposition of the fenders; under the thwarts, fore and aft, nearly up to them and for about half the length of the boat, I should lash on each side a cork float, say 12 or 15 inches in diameter, to *assist* in keeping the boat somewhat manageable when she ships water, or is stove. If we attempt to add any more extra buoyancy the boat will be too heavy to launch and to transport, and will not command the confidence of the beach men. The inside floats should be carefully covered with the best cotton canvas, so as to exclude water; they need only to be stopped to the risings, and will be very useful sometimes in sending to a wreck, or in buoying up hawsers, etc. Everything should be detachable, so that if the boat be found too heavy, a part or all can be removed without cost and put back at pleasure. This is the best and simplest compromise I can recommend for our exposed beaches, where the population is sparse.

As an experiment, I should very much like to see a boat built of light wood or iron, as full of solid cork as will be possible and admit of room for the feet of the rowers and the steersman, and have valves well up on the side, sufficiently handy for the oarsmen to open readily to let out water. The only objection to such a plan would be that the steersman must have room, not only to stand but to move round sharp, and for this he would require an open space about 4 by 2½ feet, sufficiently low down to handle his long oar. If the rest of the boat should have space only for the feet of the men, in the event of shipping water, this standing-room would be flooded and the boat would be in danger by tipping by the stern, and thus interfere with readily handling her. The only way to get over this would be to leave a space forward equal in cubic feet to the standing-room aft to counterbalance the same; these spaces being supplied with delivery valves would clear themselves of water; all this being well, we should have to encounter the chances of getting water into one space and not into the other which might occur sometimes. I am of opinion, on the whole, that these spaces could be fitted so as to relieve themselves of water almost instantly by the aid of the large mass of cork. Another difficulty, that of want of room to take in as many at the least as the crew consists of, must be met by having certain blocks, removable, so as to admit the feet of passengers; this can be easily managed, all else being well. Cork of good quality although buoyant absorbs some water, and becomes considerably heavier by immersion and by long exposure to dampness—how much I do not know; not enough I suppose to prevent its use in such a boat.

I presume that masses of cork, made to shape in sections to fit the boat up to the thwarts, could be kept dry by covering them with cotton canvas, with or without paint; but this would add to the weight and cost, and be constantly rotting. Again, it may be that the separate pieces of cork constituting the blocks could be economically cemented by marine glue or some light pigment, to keep out water from their interstices; all of which are hints worthy of consideration in applying cork to boats.

ON MEANS FOR

COMMUNICATING WITH WRECKS.

In England, the Manby mortar, fully illustrated and described in a pamphlet dated 1826, was for some time the popular means for getting communication, and in this country a similar piece of ordnance continues to be the medium, and as it is likely to be, I will say a few words as to its use. Manby's original mortar weighed, with the bed or block on which it was mounted, about 3 cwt., and was said to carry by means of a 24-lb shot, a rope of 1½ inches 200 yards, or a dep-sea line 270 yards "against the utmost power of the wind." It was also recommended as suitable to throw out a grapnel shot carrying a rope strong enough to facilitate hauling a boat through the surf. Manby also recommended and illustrated the use of a small mortar, which was exhibited to a Committee of the House of Commons, in 1814. The apparatus, including the line and frame upon which it was "faked," cartridges, tubes, port-fire, slow-match, all arranged to be slung by a strap over the shoulders, weighed only 32 lbs.; the calibre of the piece 2 lbs.; the line of the size of a "log-line" was projected 120 yards.

As "the utmost power of the wind," a rope "strong enough to haul a boat off shore," a "log-line," are very indefinite terms, no correct idea can be formed of the power of the Manby mortar from his own description. Manby connected his projectiles with the line to be thrown by tails or beckets long enough to reach two feet beyond the muzzle of the mortar, made of plaited green hide. Manby justly places great stress on the laying of the line clear for running, and illustrates several ways of doing it. One very good method, especially for preparing the line in the dark is to "fake" it back and forth over pins standing up six inches, round the edge of a frame of wood; this is an effective way of keeping the line from fouling; when made up and ready for firing, the frame is capsized, leaving the line in a pile clear for running. Manby also illustrates a pistol with a box over the lock intended to keep the powder dry ready to fire the mortar; also a shell containing inflamable matter and a fuse to be fired at night to illuminate the vicinity of the wreck, and enable the operators of the mortar to point it aright; also a shell filled with composition, attached to the line, it has four holes in the side towards the powder and in being fired is intended to throw out tails of fire, like a rocket, so that its flight to the wreck may be correctly ascertained. It is not stated that these shells were ever brought into actual practice.

Manby also illustrates a mode of placing anchors off shore outside the broken water at all stations, connected by bridles, and these supported by a buoy, so that the grapnel anchor or shot could be projected and catch on the bridle or mooring rope, and thus furnish a means for hauling the boat off. I am not aware that this idea was ever carried out; on a rocky shore, where the bottom is not subject to changes, it might answer a good purpose and is worth consideration for some localities on our coast. But, in places like the Jersey or Nantucket, or Cape Cod shores, it would be useless on account of the shifting nature of the sands, and the liability to be carried away by ice.

Manby having been long a resident on the seacoast, gives some very good general hints as to life-boats, and among other things says, in speaking of the original boat of Greathead: "She is excellent for the entrance of a harbor where there is no difficulty in launching, or the aid of sails necessary, but her size and weight would render it impossible to launch her through a heavy surf. The form is different from the boats peculiar to the coast. It is of the first importance for a life-boat to resemble as much as possible those which the pilots and beach-men are accustomed to and have confidence in, not only because it is necessary to humor the prejudices of men whose services are required, but because whatever tends to increase their confidence, must in proportion increase the chance of saving life."

Whatever may be said of the antiquated ideas of Manby, the above quotation will forever hold good. Manby also recommends all life-boats to be furnished with a short gun to throw a line from the boat to a wreck, where the nature of the case renders a very near approach difficult; I shall allude to the best means for effecting this further on. Manby also illustrates several modes of getting people on shore, after having established communication by the mortar; one is by slinging a ships' cot with the bottom opened to let out water, and another a hammock padded outside by any convenient means for protection in landing on a rocky shore; another by a snatch block and common sling. He alludes particularly to a case where the vessel cannot be reached by mortar line, or where there is no boat—the crew paying out a line by means of a cask or spar, but the undertow keeps it out of reach of persons on the beach—then some means to grapple it must come in play, either by the small mortar or the anchor shot, or by throwing out a hand line armed with hooks to catch the rope.

Lastly, Manby gives some valuable suggestions as to making signals by motions of the arms, to be recognized on board of all vessels, and by black-boards, whereon can be written in chalk certain orders as to manipulating the ropes, etc. Notwithstanding the ancient date of Manby's work, it may be read with profit. Without taking up any more time in quoting from it let me proceed to quote from the report to the Duke of Northumberland, some of its facts and suggestions as to mortars, rockets, lines, life-boat gear, etc.

Commander Jerningham's report to the Comptroller of the Coast Guard, says, in brief:

"That the experiments on Woolwich marshes gives the following results:

Range obtained by Manby mortar of brass, 5½ inch calibre, elevation 33°, charge 10 oz. powder, being the mean of 20 rounds:

In fine weather with Russia hemp line of 6-thread,	245	yds.
" " " Manilla, same size, . . .	285	"
Moderate weather, fresh breeze, hemp, . . .	237	"
" " " " Manilla, . .	279	"
Strong gale, squally, elevation 28°, hemp, . .	211	"
" " " " " Manilla,. .	243	"

He says, "a strong wind directly against the wind requires a less elevation than in moderate weather, 28° to 33° will be the best in blowy weather, and in moderate and calm weather 37°. The wind across the range will reduce the flight more than the wind directly ahead. Variation of ranges are so capricious that I have obtained the same results with 25° as 33°. The laws of projectiles require it to be kept in mind that the more horizontally the line can be fired, the less resistance.

"The quality and charge of powder, is a matter of the utmost importance; some addition must be made to the charge, when powder has been long kept in a damp boat-house.

"With reference to the charge no more than 16 oz. ought to be used in the 5½ inch brass mortar, and when the charge exceeds 12 oz. the large cylindrical shot should be used, the initial velocity being less than with a lighter shot, a manilla line laid up soft, and carefully made of best stock, will stand 16 oz., when 12 oz. will break russia hemp. The manilla lines are less liable to kink, 120 fathoms of ¾ inch line, weighing 11 lbs. against 15½ lbs. for russia hemp. I found that the lines balled up after the manner of rope-makers spun-yarn, were more portable than on racks, as in present use; were less liable to foul, and would always run out clear when taken from the heart of the ball, and require less space.

"Manilla rope beckets may be made fast directly to the shot without the intervention of hide, the latter becoming stiff and breaking frequently after being long in store. One shot was fired 27 times with the same manilla strap without any apparent damage and is much less expensive and uncertain than hide. Manilla line will bear being coiled away when wet with salt water, it is especially appropriate for the lines of communication between the shore and the wreck."

In regard to charges, he says:

"Not less than 6 oz. should be used, which in moderate weather and a 30-pound shot, will give 200 yards; where a long range is necessary, requiring two lines of 120 fathoms, a lead shot, and a becket of 1½ manilla fitted with a long running eye so as to allow of rendering, thereby obviating the sudden jerk, are requisite on the large cylindrical shot, (weight not given.) These may be fired with 16 oz. powder, and will give in moderate weather a range of 350 yards with 37° elevation and in strong winds 280, with 28° elevation.

"In case a wreck is close, the bight of a larger line, carrying a small block, may be fired off with 16 oz. I have fired many lines after being wet, as they lay on the beach, with complete success; but when time will allow, the line should be reeled into balls, and stored when dry, in canvas bags. If it is desired to illuminate the line, it can be carried in a covered tub, which being filled with oil and phosphorus will have that effect. Experiments are in progress by Lieut. Colguhoun, for effecting communication at short distances by means of a hand-rocket. I have a small hand-mortar with a shoulder stock to carry a leaden projectile and line 80 yards, as suggested by Miss Gurney, of Northrepps.

"I enclose a sketch of an anchor-shot, which, after many anxious experiments, I can recommend to stand 10 oz. powder fired from the 5½ inch mortar, with a rope of 1½, 210 yards, in moderate weather, elevation 33° and 150 in a gale. Its holding power on sandy bottom is equal to the strength of 12 men, and two such anchors would haul off any life-boat on the Eastern coast. The length of the shank is 30 inches and of the stock 26 inches, flukes 30, weight 45 lbs. In the manufacture great care is requisite that the best iron be used, it should be capable of having a knot tied in a cold bar. The principal difficulty I had to contend with was the breaking of the stock, but it was overcome, I have one now which has been fired 17 times, and is still fit for use.

"I found an ash stock stood well, but it held too much wind."

In reference to these quotations, I have to remark that in the small iron mortars of the Humane Society carrying a 12 lb. solid shot, and shell of about 9 lb., with fine manilla line of six-thread, manilla rope beckets of 1½ inch, spliced into a sunken eye in the shot and shell, and 4 ounces of powder, we have obtained in moderate weather, ranges of 200 to 250 yards with the solid shot. Against the wind, the *shell* cannot be sent so far, and its initial velocity, at the start, with 4 ounces powder is sometimes too great for the becket; but, with the wind, it will go about as far as the shot, and being less costly and lighter there is economy in it. In the only 5½ inch Manby mortar belonging to the Humane Society, presented many years ago by the Royal National Institution, we have used in experiments both solid shot and shell, and find it difficult to insure the integrity of the lanyard or becket with over 8 ounces powder. We have several new mortars of same calibre, but longer, which will bear more charge, being mounted on heavy block carriages without wheels, calculated to stand a heavy recoil. The original carriages, although carefully made at the Navy Yard, have been found too weak to withstand the recoil of 5½ inch mortars. Much depends, as Jerningham says, on the quality of the powder, in fact, next to the integrity of the lines and beckets, *this is the great point,* and one which should be carefully tested by government experts. My impression is that fine rifle powder is too sudden in its effects, and that we want coarser powder to start the heavy projectiles more gradually; but this is a question which I leave to experiments by experts. We have never attempted to fire 16 ounces powder from our heaviest mortars; the recoil, unless the block is buried in the sand, would be great, and the line or becket be sure to break. Our beaches are generally so steep that vessels come near enough to be reached with small charges, except in certain localities, as off Nausett, and Peaked Hill Bars on Cape Cod, and off some of the beaches of Nantucket and Martha's Vineyard, and in these localities the "rips" or sand bars lie too far off to be reached by any mortar. In my experience, the ball is the simplest and best way of preparing the line for a first fire, taking care to haul out two or three fathoms from the heart of the ball; after once firing, to save time the line may be ranged along the beach and will generally run out clear if carefully laid, but not so far as when dry; the becket should be wet just before putting the shot in place. We have recently had made at the Navy Yard, some rawhide selvagee beckets, carefully marled down, which so far as tried, promise well; but they must be kept supple by oil. On the whole, I am inclined to recommend the manilla becket, because it can always be fitted from the general stores in a few minutes, and it requires no special care beyond keeping dry. The running eye, to which Jerningham alludes, ought to be tested against the usual splice.

As to the means of communicating between the life-boat and the wreck, or between the shore and wreck, when near by. Various means, more simple and practicable than carrying a fire-arm, offer to my mind. A person accustomed to throw off a bluefish leaden bait, can easily throw by hand a cod-line by means of a leaden weight, 60 or eighty yards; next to this a short shoulder-piece, say of inch calibre, can throw the same line attached to a stick fitted after the French plan, to be described further on, a distance of 80 to 100 yards, according to the wind. It does not often occur that a boat cannot approach a wreck under her lee, or anchor to windward and veer down to it. Still, it is well in this discussion, to consider and to provide for all contingencies. The anchor-shot of Jerningham, and Manby's grapnel-shot deserve careful study.

Among the fittings of a station on the English coast, I find :—Transporting cart, with 120 fathoms 3-inch manilla; a whip of 1½ inch, 2 coils of 120 fathoms spliced together, rove through a 5 inch block, with its tail consisting of 4 small lines, 3 in balls and 1 in a tub; 4 round barbed shot, fitted with fuzes, weight 30 lbs; 2 cylindrical barbed shot, and two large oval long barbed shot, suspended under the axle, and 3 anchor shot in the cart; also the mortar and its bed; ammunition box to contain 8 charges of 10 ounces, 16 of 8, and 8 of 4; port-fire, slow-match, pistol and tube-box or percussion caps, water-proof cartridges, hammers, shovel, 50 fathoms 1 inch line, to be used as stray-line, to be bent on to the outer end of the small line, spunyarn, sheepskin to wipe mortar, beckets for shot, to be in the form of grommets of 1½ manilla, 1 foot long in the bight, and marled with manilla; tallies should also be attached to the cart to send off, marked, "make fast tail-block," "make fast this, and cast off whip." Full directions are given as to how to get the communication, how to make fast the shore end of the travelling rope, by converting the cart into an anchor; the plan of illuminating the line is detailed; all of which though interesting must be left to the general intelligence of operators.

As to the means used in this country for landing persons after the communication is obtained, a few words will not be amiss. A simple bowline hung to a snatch block, to travel by means of the whip or hauling line, has been used with success at Nantucket.

Recently we have adopted the Beeching cork body-buoy with canvas legs, to be hung to the travelling rope by a bridle.

Next, for certain places, and for use where large numbers, or where women and children and sick persons are to be landed, a "balsa," made up of hoops strengthened by battens and covered with canvas, with a man-hole and nozzle of canvas, strings, etc. are provided; the form is that of two cones with their bases attached; it weighs very little, and has solid ends, through which runs a bolt with an eye on the outside for the hauling lines. This machine, though never yet instrumental in saving life, has been tried and found very good to haul back and forth on the water by the whip, or by travelling on the large rope if required, all of which will depend in practice on the nature of the shore and the state of the weather; ordinarily, on a sand beach, two persons could be got on shore dry in it with ease through a heavy surf, without risk of fracture. The persons being placed in it, could draw in the canvas nozzle and tie it, or hold it in their hands, or it can be tied outside, after placing them. This is a cheap and very effective vehicle, much easier to handle than our Francis metallic cars, about 8 or 10 feet long and weighing some 400 or 500 lbs. Although it appears to be in use, I do not remember to have seen any detailed account of the performance of the anchor-shot in England.

My attention was called about two years ago to the inventions of Mr. John B. Rogers, of London, for saving life, the principal feature of which is a projectile anchor, said to weigh 112 lbs.; it has three folding flukes, and is to be fired like Jerningham's; it has attached to it a block of peculiar construction, said to be free from all danger of choking by weeds, etc.; this block is to be carried with the anchor and a whip or hauling line to the wreck, without the intervention and loss of time by getting off a small line by mortar or rocket, or the anchor is to be planted outside the surf, to haul out a boat. Mr. Rogers also has a cone-shaped projectile of wood, to be thrown with the block, when not necessary to throw the anchor.

In January, 1870, as I learn through an exhaustive list of testimonials contained in a pamphlet on Rogers' projectile anchor, an experiment was made under the auspices of the Admiralty; the article says; "with the exception of one or two slight defects in the construction, which can be easily remedied, the trial was attended with complete success, and has firmly established the value of the anchor, the weight of which, thrown from an 8 inch mortar, with 12 ounces of large grain powder, was 134 lbs., and with block and line, 200, the range was 134 yards and 2 feet."

Another interesting trial took place in April, under Mr. Rogers's own eye, when it is said the anchor was successfully projected from a common howitzer. Again in June, experiments were made at Portsmouth, under the supervision of Capt. Boys, of the Excellent.

The article from the Times, June 2, 1870, says:

"An 8 inch ordinary mortar was used; in the first experiment a projectile anchor weighing 128 lbs., with an expansive block, and a line of one inch rove in the block, was carried 156 yards with 8 oz. powder, and by these means a 3½ inch hawser was passed as a continuous rope. In the second experiment, it was sent with the same charge and an elevation of 38°, 152 yards from the shore, by this the hawser was hauled off to the anchor and the ship's launch and 10 men not assisting, were hauled off without tripping the anchor. In the third experiment, the cone and block were thrown with same charge 163 yards. In the fourth experiment, 12 oz. threw the cone and block 217 yards; an inch rope was used in each case."

The Army and Navy Gazette, says, under date Sept. 10, 1870: "that the Lords of the Admiralty have given Mr. Rogers £200 towards his expenses in testing the merits of his invention."

The Liverpool Courier, of Oct. 1, 1870, says, "that a large party went down the river to see Mr. Rogers experiment with his cone and a line of one inch, the first shot out of a little 3½ inch mortar firing a 12 lb. projectile with 2 oz. powder and an elevation of 45°, sent the cone up 150 yards, and it fell at 80 from the operating steamer. It was again tried at a low elevation with the same charge, and then carried the cone and line 200 yards. On the third trial *a very light line* was sent in a straight line upwards of 400 yards, but the line fouling broke and the cone and block were lost."

The Daily Post, of Liverpool, 3d Oct., gives the first shot at 200 yards up, and considered it a valuable test of the power to get a line up a cliff, the second shot at 250, and at the third fire *with more powder* and a finer line, it went 400 yards, this account states that the *model mortar* weighing 8 lbs., threw a 3 pound projectile and line 80 yards with a thimble full of powder.

The coxswain and crew of a life-boat at New Brighton, having seen the experiments, say: "we consider the invention far superior to the present rocket system."

In Nov. 1870, at a meeting of the Royal Naval Reserve Club, Mark Lane, sundry resolves were agreed on, from which I quote only one: "considering the number and variety of experiments this invention has gone through, with the sanction and approval (and the assistance) of the Admiralty, this meeting strongly recommend its adoption by that excellent and valuable body known as the Royal National Life-boat Institution."

In December the Shipping and Mercantile Gazette, says: "a final trial of Rogers process will take place at Shoeburyness shortly, at the expense of the Board of Trade."

On receiving the above important facts the Humane Society of Massachusetts, took measures to try Rogers apparatus and procured permission to have it done "*Secundum artem*" at the Watertown Arsenal, the writer requested Mr. Rogers to ship per United States Ship Worcester when she returned from her mission of mercy, a perfect sample of the apparatus, but it was never sent.

In answer to my inquiries as to the Rogers anchor, Captain J. R. Ward, Inspector of the Royal National Society, informed me on the 31st January, 1871, that a trial would be made at Shoeburyness, as above stated. I have never been informed of the result of that trial, if it took place. Captain Ward, who has had great experience in life saving means, expresses the opinion that the Rogers apparatus will not take the place of the Boxer rocket, nor does he think it desirable to throw off a double line and block in preference to a single one; the anchor shot he thinks would be very likely to attach itself in the wrong place.

Captain Ward also says that where the boats of the Royal Institution are not locomotive by land, they have permanent anchors and warps laid down during the winter months, and where there are transporting carriages, they can be launched from them without the aid of an anchor, and where the shore is flat, anchors would be of no use, as they could not be thrown far enough to haul a boat through the surf. He says, also, that Rogers succeeds in throwing an anchor by a 70 lb. mortar to a much greater distance with the block and double line than he expected. I shall take measures to ascertain the result of the experiments at Shoeburyness. The testimony I have quoted above still leaves a considerable margin to hope that the Rogers anchor may be utilized in this country where we have no Boxer rocket apparatus.

THE BOXER ROCKET.

I learn from a letter of Thomas Gray, Esq., Secretary of the Board of Trade, Whitehall, London, of date 12th June, 1867, that the Manby mortar has "been almost entirely superseded by the rocket, designed by Lieut.-Col. Boxer, R. A., of the Royal Laboratory, Woolwich. It consists of two rockets arranged end on to each other in one case. The effect is that on the first rocket being expended, after reaching a certain distance, the second takes fire and completes the range. With it is used a line made of Italian hemp, of 500 yards, weighing 46 lbs." With the letter from which I have quoted, there came drawings of the rocket and apparatus, as well as a book of instructions for the use thereof, from which I extract a portion, showing how completely the organization is carried out.

"The inspecting officer of coast guard is responsible for the efficiency of the mortar and rocket in his division. They are inspected and exercised once a quarter; one or two, but not more than four shots may be fired, and the whole operation of setting up a hawser and hauling persons to and from a tree or flag staff to be gone through. Annual report to be made by inspectors to the Board of Trade. The number of rockets to each apparatus is 18; lines, 2 or more."

The apparatus is described as hereunder.

"A spring cart with broad or narrow tires, to suit the coast, fitted with lamps, drag ropes similar to field artillery, box with stores, and a water-tight compartment for carrying the rockets, crutches for the tubes, staves and triangle, boxes with faking pins for the lines, a 3 inch manilla hawser 40 to 120 fathoms, according to the steepness of the shore, a whip 1½ inch manilla, double the length of the hawser, rove through a block with a tail of two fathoms, the ends of whip spliced together so as to make an endless rope."

Here let me say, the block should have a swallow large enough to pass freely a snug eye-splice, to be made in each end of the whip, whereby the turns can be taken out the more readily and the whip spread along the shore; if spliced together to make a permanent and continuous rope as above quoted, the whip will be likely to get full of kinks.

To go on with the abbreviated instructions: "a slung buoy with petticoat breeches, in which to place a person to be hauled on shore; a traveller or inverted block attached to the buoy to carry it along the hawser by the whip or hauling line." Note.—I have adopted for this traveller an iron ring and eye, the ring covered with trucks so that it cannot well choke by seaweed, ice, etc. This I consider better than a block. "a tackle for setting up the hawser, 3 small spars arranged for a triangle to raise the hawser clear of the crest of the waves, an anchor with one fluke, whereby to set up the hawser—a good substitute is a plank with a piece of chain to be buried in the sand or earth, a red flag and staff, and a lantern with a red lens, two spades, a shovel and pick, a selvagee strap, a light hand-barrow; three sets of tally-boards, 9 by 5 inches, with directions (written in French and English,) to be sent off to the wreck." NOTE.—In some cases we have used india rubber pocket books with parchment tallies in them, and in other cases a strong bottle has been sent off by the small line with directions to await the fall of the tide or the coming of the boat, etc. "Long light of Boxer's 1 box, 18 signal rockets showing white and red stars, 2 heaving sticks with lines." NOTE.—A bluefish line and its leaden bait and hook can be thrown 80 yards or more. "A hawser cutter, a tarpaulin to cover the cart and to lay on the beach to coil the whip on, two of Capt. Ward's life-belts, and two life-lines." NOTE.—All the rockets and illuminating gear with mortars, powder, shot, etc., are supplied by the War Department. "The mortar fittings consist of, mortar 5½ inch, bed, round 24-lb. shot, oblong 24, with fuzes, copper friction-tubes, and L. G. powder."

As space does not admit of recapitulating all the details contained in the book of instructions, I shall content myself with extracting only sufficient to turn attention in the right direction.

"Eight men required for full drill of the rocket apparatus, hawser, lines, etc., four of these belong to Coast Guard attached to station, the rest called from other stations or volunteers; exercise to be on shore, so as to recover the shot, measure range, etc.; Coast Guard men not paid for exercise, unless they travel over four miles, for the excess three pence a mile paid. Under the Shipping Act, horses and carts can be taken, but it is best to understand with near residents as to loan of these in case of emergency. The Inspector or Custom's Officer, has power to command all present to assist at a rescue, any one refusing can be made to pay £50. The elevation of the Boxer tube to be 35 to 38 degrees, depending on the wind. The first shot to be fired from the box, tilted in the direction of the wreck; afterwards, to save time, from the beach; great care necessary for first shot, as a wet and dirty line does not go so well."

Here follow details as to the management in getting off the hawser, etc.

Remuneration to Coast Guard men, etc.:

"When going to a wreck and *saving life*, 2 shillings to each, otherwise, 1 shilling. In cases of special importance, if the inspector approves, more will be paid, others assisting may be recommended for pay. Chief officers at stations paid double the men when assisting at a wreck. In no case where lives are saved by apparatus is salvage to be claimed on the ship. Volunteer companies to be encouraged and assisted by Coast Guard. To these apparatus will be found, rent of house paid, and remuneration awarded by the Board of Trade, according to the circumstances of rescue, perfection of drill, etc. Volunteer brigades to be subject to order of the Senior Officer of Coast Guard, if present, or Senior Custom Officer; in their absence, to the Senior Officer of the brigade. Rates of pay for volunteers, for exercise, 2 shillings each, and at wrecks, from 2 shillings and 6 pence to £1, according to circumstances, the limit as to the number in each case, 25." Here follow details as to the drill of rocket brigade, too long to copy, but from which the following brief hints are extracted.

"Coast Guard stations occur all along the coast, fire guns by day, or burn lights or rockets by night, to call the crews. Each man works by his number in moving to the scene of wreck, similar to the drill of guns in vessels of war; every man has his special duty to do; many stations having old men-of-war's men, use the boatswain's call in drill and service."

I have before me a detailed drawing of the Boxer accelerating rocket and fittings, from which is seen that the details are most carefully got up. There are plain drawings of all the parts and of the manner of manipulating them. The explanation warrants some further notice. It is "A compound rocket, so arranged that when the first rocket has expended its force, the second is ignited and gives a new impulse. By this arrangement of the force an increased range is obtained without breaking the line, (which would occur if the force of the two were applied to the first start.) The line is attached to the stick, passing along the side of the rocket case, by a knot in the end, which passes through india rubber washers; this relieves the sudden shock of the start. The rocket is fired both by a lock attached near the tail of the case, or by a fuze and port-fire. The ignition of the second charge should take place when the rocket has reached the highest point of the trajectory, or just beyond it."

I have been thus particular in describing the Boxer rocket, because I desire to call the attention of our legislators and governors and their servants to the importance, as we progress in the scale of nations, of inaugurating the best means in use in older countries for diminishing the dangers of the sea. I would also call the attention of the government to the propriety of striking off a suitable medal to be awarded to all who may have the good fortune of distinguishing themselves through the instrumentalities afforded by the government stations.

"Victoria, by the grace of God, etc., etc.," in 1866, instituted a decoration styled the Albert Medal, a gold oval-shaped badge inscribed "for gallantry in saving life at sea," to be given upon the recommendation of the Board of Trade. It is wisely provided that if any one holding the decoration shall be guilty, in the opinion of the Queen, of any conduct which ought to disqualify him from holding the badge, it shall be forfeited, and every person before receiving it shall enter into a contract to return it if called for. This is an example worthy of imitation by our government.

This book of instructions, from which I have made such liberal extracts, closes by giving directions for restoring suspended animation, by Drs. Marshall Hall, and H. R. Silvester's methods, with illustrations of the manner of handling the body. These instructions are posted at all the stations and circulate throughout the country and colonies and in the navy and coast guard service.

The Humane Society of Massachusetts would long since have adopted the Boxer rocket if it could have afforded means for buying, drilling and keeping the apparatus in order. It will be found much more portable than the mortar apparatus and has a longer range and can be seen in its flight at night, when a shot or shell cannot, unless the latter be filled with some inflammable material. The use of the rocket is held under letters patent in England and can only be procured from the manufacturers, with whom Col. Boxer has bargained for its use.

The cost of a complete set of Boxer rocket apparatus, as I learned in 1867 from the manufacturers, J. & A. W. Birt, Dock Street, Nos. 3 and 4, London, as per list: 24 rockets and sticks, 20 lights, 20 port-fires, 24 primers, 28 port-fire primers, handles, 3 lines, 3 line-boxes, whip and hawser, tally-boards, blocks, sling-buoy, triangle, 2 Ward belts, and life-lines, flag, lantern, tarpaulin, anchor, axe, spade, hand-barrow, straps, 36 tubes detonating, 36 fuzes, 74 washers, 36 pins, rocket-frame, diagrams, and packing, is £125 cash, exclusive of the shipping charges.

Some correspondence was had with the U. S. War Department, on the subject of making the Boxer rocket at the U. S. Laboratories, after procuring permission from Col. Boxer. Major Gen. Dyer, Chief of Ordnance informed me Aug. 5, 1867, that if we could not get them made by private parties, an order would be given to make them at Watertown, but as Col. Boxer had arranged his business with the Birts, for the manufacture and sale, nothing further could be done, than to import a set; this the Humane Society was not in a condition to do; or was not called on to do by reason of my absence for two years in Europe.

For many years the Dennett rocket was used in England, and it was tried here by the Humane Society, but it was found to deteriorate very much when exposed to the changes of climate and sometimes it bursts prematurely; its use has therefore been discontinued, the Boxer rocket costs in England about ten shillings, rendering it expensive to exercise on a large scale.

I will now proceed to speak on the subject of

Instructions for the Organization and Management of the Life-boat and Mortar Apparatus of the Royal National Institution of Great Britain.

Without organization all our efforts in the direction of saving life will be feeble or useless; unless the establishments lately decided on, upon our coasts under the préstige of the Government, are to be cared for, by well paid competent men, they will prove failures. In the discussion of this subject we may get some valuable hints from the rules of the Royal Society. I shall therefore quote liberally from the regulations of that body, date 1860.

"1st. The crew of a first-class boat consists of first and second coxswain, bowman, and as many oarsmen as there are oars.

"2nd. For every boat an equal number are enrolled, the first to form the regular crew and the rest to fill vacancies and absences.

"3rd. They are to consist of men living near by.

"4th. Salary of first coxswain £8 per annum. When required to go afloat to save life, they will receive 10 shillings by day, and £1 at night, and for going on exercise, 5 shillings in rough weather, and 3 shillings for smooth.

"5th. If money be received as salvage of property two shares to be reserved for the local committee, for the maintenance and repair of the boat, the remainder to be divided among the coxswains and crew. If the salvage paid be for the saving of life, no portion to go to the crew."

A note to this says: "Salvage for saving life shall be, according to Shipping Act of 1854, Section 459, payable by owners prior to any other claim; but as the life-boat crew are paid by the Society, it is desirable that no demand be made except under extraordinary circumstances and the sanction of the Central Committee obtained."

" 6th. If local rewards are obtained for special acts of gallantry it is recommended that the award be paid to the crew.

"7th. At each station is a local Committee to govern the movements of the boat.

" 8th. The boat to be put afloat for exercise once a quarter; preference to be given to rough weather.

"9th. Committee to make quarterly report in regard to condition of apparatus.

"10th. Boat to be kept on her carriage in boat-house with all gear except perishable articles which must be secured from damp.

" 11th. Three keys kept in different places with the address painted on the door, one with coxswain, and two with the local Committee.

" 12th. In the event of a call, coxswain assembles his crew, and if any are absent he is to call for volunteers, to be paid like the crew.

" 13th. If the wreck is distant the coxswain to press horses into service.

" 14th. Reward of 7 shillings to the first man who brings news of a wreck out of sight of the station."

15th. As to signals by day and night to call crew.

16th. As to manner of boarding the wreck.

" 17th. On boarding, the saving of life *to be the first and sole consideration.* No goods or baggage to be put in to the danger of the boat.

" 18th. On landing men from wreck, notice to be given to the 'Fisherman's and Mariner's Benevolent Society.'

"19th. No one to leave in a life-boat except the crew or by the sanction of Committee

"20th. Boat not to be used to take off an anchor, nor for salvage of property, stores, pilot, or orders, so as to interfere with private enterprise, except by permission of Committee.

"21st. Relates to the preparations to be made by the coxswain when the weather looks bad.

"22nd. In winter, in certain places, it is recommended to place an anchor off shore with buoy and line ready to haul off the boat.

"23d. Coxswain to keep a journal to be sent after each service on wreck to the Society in London.

"24th. Instructions and illustrations for restoring suspended animation to be posted in boat-house and to be always carried in the boat.

"25th. On returning from service the boat to be hauled up, and the first fine day examined, dried, etc.

"26th. Coxswain held responsible for the efficiency and good order of his boat and gear."

The above general regulations are very much curtailed, others are given as to the time of painting, inspection after winter, etc., etc.

The gear of a life-boat consists of:

1st. For 32 foot boats, anchor 75 lbs., secured to the platform of the boat; cable 60 fathoms, 3½ inch.

2nd. Grapnel 25 lbs.

3d. Spring for cable.

4th. A norman to ship in step of mast for towing, or riding at anchor.

5th. Set of oars with lanyards, and a spare oar for every two men.

6th. Iron thole-pins, grommets, and spare ones.

7th. Two steering oars, and two boat-hooks.

8th. Two hand-grapnels, and heaving-lines.

9th. One axe, and two hatchets in each boat.

10th. Life-buoy and line of 1½ manilla lines over the side knotted, for life-lines.

11th. Boat compass and binnacle where necessary.

12th. Spy-glass, port-fires, Lantern, etc.

13th. Hand-rockets for throwing line to wreck.

14th. Hand lead and line.

15th. Hammer and nails, sheet lead, chisel, marline-spike, grease, oakum, etc.

16th. Cork belt for every one of crew.

17th. Keg of water.

18th. Boat-carriage, and gear.

19th. Chest of small stores.

20th. Mast, Sails, etc.

Rafts and General Means, for Saving Life at Sea and on Shore.

1st. Within my experience comes the raft, called by its present owners, the "Monitor Raft," originally known as the Perry Raft.

A three cylinder raft went to England under sail, leaving New York June 12, 1867, arriving, July 25.

The raft consists of two or more air-tight cylinders, incased in heavy canvas and connected by canvas flanges forming when inflated a sort of deck, the whole distended into shape by a frame of wood and thwarts, and so arranged that it can be put together and inflated by an inexperienced crew after once seeing it done, in eight minutes, and the air let out and packed in about the same time, the time of inflating may be shortened by having larger valves and bellows, an experienced crew can inflate it in less time. The vulcanized rubber cylinders are the reservoir, the canvas is mainly for protecting them, and preventing rupture. It is very compact when made up and can be thrown over board from a high vessel without injury.

The following extracts from my report of a trial in Sept., 1870, will show that I have perfect confidence in the Monitor raft.

Extracts from Report to Humane Society.

I have recently tried the monitor raft sent by W. C. Thompson, President of Raft Company, and have accepted it. I went first to Provincetown, in the Revenue Cutter Vigilant, exercising the men on the way in preparing and packing the machine. About eight minutes are required to inflate the cylinders and get ready to launch, and about the same time to let out the air and pack up. On arrival at Provincetown, the raft was inflated, thrown overboard, and thirteen men landed on the beach, pulling six oars, and the raft was packed and carted over to the shore near to Peaked Hill Bars, inflated in seven minutes, and put off the beach with an officer and six men of the cutter's crew, the sea was not rough enough to make this a fair trial of the utility of the raft. I also manned it with seven men *of the locality*, and they shoved off and went through and beyond the breakers on the bars and landed much pleased with the performance; the cutter's crew manned it again, and shoved off and pulled round to Herring Cove, along shore eight or nine miles, within the outer breakers, until they met the cutter, while I drove along shore to see the performance.

Not deeming the surf sufficient at Cape Cod, I proceeded to Nantucket, arriving off the Bar on the 8th. We launched the raft and proceeded for the shore, accompanied by a whaleboat manned by Nantucket men. In pulling in about three miles the whaleboat beat the raft about one-third, showing very fair speed for the latter.

The raft was immediately landed, rolled up, put on a cart and taken to the South Shore, where we found a heavy surf; inflated the raft, with *new hands*, in about eight minutes, and having fully stated its qualities, *according to the theory given in books*, I called for volunteers to man it and go through the heavy breakers. After a good deal of delay, and with expressions of confidence in its safety by myself, as well as by Mr. Wilson, who was sent on by the raft company to teach us how to use it, only three men came forward! It was quite clear that while neither the agent *or myself* were ready to lead a crew, the beach-men of Nantucket would not have confidence enough to push off. The surf was large and ran very furiously, frequently breaking from one-quarter to one-half a mile off the beach. I had great doubt if any of the surf-boats, dories, or life-boats, would have ventured to launch in such a surf, unless prompted by an earnest desire to save life, *or to establish the first claim to a rich salvage from a wreck.* The trial was therefore abandoned for that day, and the considerable crowd returned disappointed to the city. On the 9th, arrangements were made for a crew, and we went again to the South Shore. The surf was considerably less than the day before, but still running too high to permit of any of the habitual fishermen going off *on their daily work in dories.* I induced a young man named Gardner to carry off a tub of whale-line, two hundred fathoms, and plant two dory anchors outside the inner rollers. After a delay of nearly half an hour, watching for a smooth time, the little shell was pushed off, and gallantly riding over the smooth rollers, planted the anchors and returned safely to the shore with the end of the whale line. The operation was very exciting; sometimes the dory would meet a roller and jump it, just as it was going to curl over, and disappear behind it, and again, she would wait or back in a little and allow a huge breaker to spend itself outside of her. In coming in, a wave ran her up within reach of the men on the beach, when she was hauled up. Having now established a line, it was rove through a block at each end of the raft and the slack line hauled in; one man got upon the raft, and five or six others watching a chance, it was shoved off and easily hanled beyond the regular surf *by this one man*, and again landed; then the whole crew got on it, seven in number, and hauled off and on, gradually getting confidence, until very soon they purposely veered in, so as to receive the worst "coamers," then I ordered them to weigh the anchor, and permit the raft to drift in *without any guidance from oar or rope*, the people on the beach merely hauling in the slack of the rope; she came, sometimes taking the surf on her end and sometimes on her side; finally, she was thrown high up by a huge roller, and as her stern touched the sand, the bow flew round and the men were thoroughly drenched by the curl of the surf, but all held on securely and seemed to like it. As soon as she touched the beach all hands jumped off, and assisted by willing hands, hauled the raft up.

Every man present felt convinced that no life-boat could have been submitted to such an ordeal without being rolled over and over. It was made clear that the raft cannot be upset nor submerged by any amount of sea.—Speed in *surf-boats and dories* is essential to safety, as they must be able to meet and to retreat quickly from coming rollers. The raft does not need speed; once clear of the sand, she can go ahead safely, *without paying any attention to the coming breaker*. I do not mean to say, that it would always be expedient to wet the crew, when by delay, or quickly going ahead or astern, a breaker might be avoided; but I mean to say, that nothing more than a wetting would result from meeting the crest of a very large breaker.

The reasons for not going off and on under oars, were, first, that the rowlocks and steering-oar, as well as the seats, are too low to permit of laying out full power, and next, the men were thoroughly wet and had no change of clothes at hand.

Necessary alterations in the rowlocks and the seats will be made, and a surf-boat on hand for a competitive trial, if a good surf exists.

I think the raft can carry out an anchor of 1,000 to 1,500 lbs. and a lot of stout hawser, with a crew of seven men, or if a hauling line be first established, with only men enough to tip off the anchor from a lifting plank. If this can be demonstrated, the raft will become a very popular institution with wreckers as well as humanitarians.

In continuation of my report I have to say, I went to Nantucket, and on the 23d launched the monitor raft through a considerable surf and relanded safely, carrying an anchor weighing over 1200 lbs. besides the stock. No surf boat could have done it, none would attempt it. The raft was manned by seven experienced surf-men and was hauled off by the aid of a whale line and a small anchor planted outside the breakers. After landing the anchor the raft was again launched and rowed to the westward, where a heavier surf prevailed and was manœuvred in it sufficiently to establish the fact in the minds of all present that it can do safely what no surf-boat can do.

The prospectus of the Raft Company furnishes ample evidence of its utility, by naval officers and others. A letter from J. W. Smith, Commander of the Santiago de Cuba, says, while laying off Graytown: "December 11, 1866, 4, P. M., launched raft and sent 25 soldiers on it *with knapsacks and four days rations* to land on the beach. The Norther had increased and the sea and surf were violent, all landed safely, not even getting wet, though the beach was steep and the surf running fearfully high, at dark the gale increased; I ran the ship three miles out to sea and anchored, not thinking they would attempt to bring off the raft; but to my surprise, at 9, P. M., the raft was alongside, *four men and an officer, pulling dead to windward, through a heavy sea in a gale of wind.* It is compact, can be stowed in small space, and made ready in six minutes, five men can launch it, and it can carry 40 with ease."

A still stronger testimonial of its utility in a high surf is found in a letter of C. C. Comstock, Commander of the Golden City, Pacific Mail Steamer lost on the coast of California, he writes; "I take great pleasure in reporting the great efficiency of the Monitor raft in saving life and property from the wreck of the Golden City. It forms a part of the equipment of all the P. M. Steamers, and proved much more efficient than the boats and was used in preference for landing the sick and aged, all of whom were landed without being wet, there being considerable surf at the time. Upon return trips the life-boats were, by the aid of twenty men, launched through the surf with great difficulty, while the raft drawing only two or three inches, was got off easily and made two trips to one of the boats.

We spent about thirty days at the wreck working in the surf, in which time nearly all the boats were stove and rendered useless, while the raft at the close was in as good order as at first, its elastic nature enabling it to stand the shocks which stove the boats.

In sending the boats to intercept steamers to obtain relief, the surf being high, it was only with great difficulty and danger that we could get outside the breakers, on these occasions the raft accompanied them as a precaution to pick up the crew.

"From what I have experienced I would much rather take my chance on a raft than in a life-boat, and I do not consider any vessel complete in her life saving equipments without your invaluable raft."

With all this incontestible evidence before us, I cannot understand why the Monitor raft has not become a more popular institution, unless it be on account of the cost which is $450 or $500 for one of two cylinders; a good life-boat, suitable for a large steamer and capable of carrying less safely, one-third less men, will cost nearly as much.

The only defect I found on trial which was easily remedied was that the rowlocks were too low, and the steering oar not well arranged. I am assured by Capt. Thompson, the President of the Raft Co., that a raft sent home from the Pacific for repairs after six years service, required only a small expense to render it as good as new.

There is in use a metallic raft, one of which was on board the Metis, recently wrecked, under circumstances when it ought to have been of great use; but, as I have seen no particular notice of its doings on that occasion and as none of the evidence made public alludes to the raft, the inference is not favorable, not knowing anything as to its weight and construction, I cannot speak knowingly as to its qualities.

Among the valuable contributions for floating power my attention has been called to the "Greene's patent, Nautilus or Life-Preserving Mattress." It consists of a mattress made of cork with a hole in the centre, usually filled up by a hair cushion, this hole is large enough to enable a full grown person by the help of a suspensory band to sit comfortably, head and shoulders above water. A similar machine having a joint in the centre, and a hole in the middle, so as to double down behind and before a person like a South American Poncho, and filled with granulated cork, has been long in use in England. Either of these machines would prove very valuable on board of vessels in cases of emergency like that of the Metis, and Bienville, and on board the Bristol had she been wrecked at sea; but they will not be adopted unless it can be shown that they can be furnished cheaper than a mattress filled with pig's hair, corn husks, or excelsior fibre. Next to this bed, I recommend all steam-ships to be furnished with doors to unship easily, and to have an ornamental metallic panel in them and handles to hold on by, and to make saloon decks detachable. If properly braced and made buoyant by air-cases, or cork fillings between the carlines, they will tend to save life, perhaps long enough to find succor, especially now that we have steamers leaving the United States and Europe, about every eight hours. Among the life saving means adopted in Europe, on which I have already enlarged; the French stand second only to Great Britain in the number and efficiency of their organizations.

The "Société Centrale de Sauvetage dés Naufragés," dates back only to 1865, when there were a few life-boats on the coast of France, supported by private associations. The present society is mostly supported by private contributions, as is the English institution, and like that it has considerable help from the government, in the loan or gift of arms. Like the English institution, it is patronized extensively by the government, the honorary presidents being three of the ministers; the president is an admiral, and the vice-presidents were, in July, 1872, cardinals, dukes, etc. Many notable names are found in the long list of the counsel. The work, as elsewhere, is done by the secretary, M. C. Doré. In the July number of the "Annales du Sauvetage Maritime" I find that there are 48 life-boat stations and 139 where the "porte-ammares" are located. Since the commencement the number of lives saved is 667, and the number saved by means outside the society, where rewards have been given, was 117, making 784. The expenses to the date named, were 867,764 francs, and are estimated at 150,000 per annum.

The engines or ordnance for casting lines to get communication with a wreck consist of,—the "mousketon" or carbine, whereby a line of about one-eighth of an inch in diameter is projected 80 to 100 yards, by means of a stick fitting the bore of the arm loosely, it is protected by brass ferrules at the ends, and projects several inches from the muzzle; a "coulant" or sliding becket is placed on the stick before inserting it, outside the muzzle, and to this becket the line is attached, and is carried ready for running in a small box suspended to the shoulder. The carbine is loaded in the usual way. For firing short ranges, as in rescuing a person in the surf near by, small cork floats are attached to the line; these of course reduce the flight, but have been found useful in rescuing persons. These "mousketons" are placed in charge of all coast guard, custom house, and light house keepers, and have saved many lives.

The arrangement may be utilized for getting communication from boats or from the shore to wrecks, and with some modifications, will be found very useful for tug-boats in getting their lines to vessels in rough waters.

Next comes the "espingole" or blunderbuss, weighing about forty pounds, and about one pound calibre. This is intended to be fired from any convenient place where the swivel or standard can be shipped; it is about a yard long, and carries both wooden and iron "flèches" or arrows. The wooden arrows may, in case of the line breaking, go 600 metres, and the iron ones 1,000, rendering care necessary in exercising. Ordinarily, the flight with wood is about 200 yards, and with iron 250, carrying the line.

Next comes the "perrier" or swivel gun, weighing about 80 kilogrammes and over a yard long. These guns are supplied by the government from old stocks in the arsenals, but are not so well adapted to the end desired as the new piece of Mr. August Delvigne, which will be presently described. The perrier is of calibre about four pound.

It was found, after a long course of experiments by Mons. Delvigne, and by the government, that the flèche could be fired with good effect out of any small gun, whether smooth bore or rifled, and that his system for loading any gun carrying a heavy projectile compared to the diameter of the bore, was the best.

This system consists in placing in the gun, which has no chamber, a disk of light wood and paper, so that the powder shall not reach the bottom of the bore by about three inches, the powder is contained in a case, with a wooden sabot outside of it, and the vent is so arranged that the powder is fired at about one-third the length of cartridge *from the outer end.* This arrangement causes the sudden shock which would otherwise be given to the projectile, to be more gradual in starting it, and the chances of breaking the line are diminished.

This is well illustrated in the following extract from a work by Delvigne. He quotes experiments made by the government in order to test his theory of a vacant space behind the cartridge. "Six ordinary brass thirty pound marine guns of the same size and make were tried; two were charged as usual, namely, with 7½ kilogrammes (about 15 pounds,) powder and a heavy elongated projectile of 45 kilogrammes, or nearly 90 pounds; this burst the gun at the eleventh fire. The second burst at the twelfth. One charged according to my plan with the vacant space and the same amount of powder and projectile stood 178 fires; one, 167; these had a vacant space equal to 16 centimetres; two others with this space 20 centimetres, stood 162 and 108 discharges respectively, the aggregate of which is 27 to 1 in favor of the space."

The perrier is fired simply by elevating it on a frame something like a saw-horse, leaving the breech of the gun on the soil.

The new piece of ordnance got up by Delvigne, weighs only 20 kilos., is made of gun metal, almost a straight cylinder, about 18 inches long, and has an iron tail-piece screwed into the breech and pointed, so that in firing it is simply thrust into the soil until the square breech brings up; the elevation is regulated by a quadrant and plummet put into the muzzle, the bore is about 1¼ inch, or half that of the perrier, the piece carries wooden arrows, fitted with an iron tail to reach the charge, and at the muzzle these are much larger than the tail-piece, so that the shock of the explosion operates on the square base of the arrow which is protected by a ring of metal. In loading this piece a vacant space is left as in the others, and the cartridge is fired near its outer end; the piece being very short, this brings the vent about in the centre of the length. The iron arrows are about one-third longer than the gun, and about half the length of the arrow is in the gun when ready to fire. The advantages claimed by Delvigne in this little piece over the long perrier and espingole are its cheapness and portability, while with sufficient charge it gives an equal or better range; besides the wooden and iron arrows he fires a wooden arrow out of the perrier or almost any gun, which has cross bars of round iron made malleable to resist the shock; these cross pieces are fixed at right angles to the arrow, near the outer end, and are about as long as three diameters of the arrow. It is found that in firing this, the cross pieces are bent to an angle of about forty-five degrees with the plane of the arrow, and thus form an anchor or grapnel, useful for many purposes. I saw one projected at Vincennes about two hundred yards from a four pound rifle gun, which held on to the soil sufficiently to have broken the line of about inch stuff.

Having briefly described the various arms in use in France for casting lines, it becomes necessary to go a little into detail as to the means of attaching the lines, which without due knowledge and practice of the system, will be quite useless.

The wooden "flêches" or arrows, are made both round and eight-square, the former must be accurately turned, and the latter planed true, therefore, the latter are more simple and easy to make on board ship or on shore. The "coulant," or literally *slider*, consists of half a dozen turns of line put on something, as a whipping is put on a rope, only the ends overlaid by the rest must be left out, so that the turns can easily be pulled taut; much depends on this being done right; if the turns are too tight, the becket with its double bight and the line moves too slowly, and the "coulant" jams half way, causing the flêche to wabble and turn over; and if put on too loose, it runs down when the gun is fired, so fast as to break when it arrives at the projecting ferrule at the base. It is not too much to say that all depends on this being done right; the flêche should be slightly greased and the line either fired from a ball, or from the ground, as in the mortar exercise. Practice has made this so perfect that in France failures seldom occur from this cause. Arrows of wood have the advantage of floating if they drop near the wreck, and of being readily recovered when they go beyond or fall far short. The iron flêche is intended for long ranges or strong contrary winds. The distance depends so much on weather, on the amount of charge, elevation, and the line running clear, that I will only say it varies from 180 to 350 metres.

The system is worth study by every navigator, and in war ships where the drill can be made perfect, and where there always are or should be guns of small calibre, and material for fléches and lines, it will prove of great value for communicating with wrecks, with the shore, or with vessels afloat. The rifled twelve pound boat gun is perfectly adapted for throwing a stick as long as a common handspike. Even for army purposes, it would be very useful for throwing a line across streams in aid of pontoon movements, etc., and in fire brigades on shore, a small gun and stout line would often come in play to communicate with high buildings, so that rope or other ladders could be got up.

In regard to the vacant space behind heavy projectiles, which Delvigne claims to start them more gradually, I would suggest that the system might be found valuable for military purposes, when firing heavy projectiles out of such guns as the hundred pound Parrot guns,—but this is treading on ground where I am a green hand. I should have said further back in regard to the small new gun, that besides using it by thrusting the tail into the soil, it is mounted in a moment for service, *where the ground is hard,* on a simple block, which can be elevated by simply blocking up.

We have a melancholy catalogue of wrecks and losses of lives, which have occurred within the last twenty years, among which I recall among the most prominent,—the Amazon; the Connaught, destroyed on the Atlantic; the Ocean Monarch, off Liverpool; the Bienville and the America by fire; the Birkenhead, off the Cape of Good Hope; the Caledonia, emigrant ship; the Arctic, Capt. Luce, off the coast of Newfoundland; the City of Bath, off Hatteras; the Charles Bartlett, emigrant ship; Atlantic, on Lake Erie; the Northern Light, sailing ship; the Pacific, Capt. Eldridge; the steamer Golden City, in California; the Atlantic, near

Fisher's Island Sound; the Royal Charter, coast of Ireland; the Henry Clay, burned on the North River; the William Penn, off Hatteras; and among vessels of war, the frigate Bombay, in La Plata; a Russian liner, in the Baltic, not long ago; the Captain; one of our Monitors, off Charleston; the Oneida, Japan; and a host of others on the ocean, lakes, and rivers, too numerous to mention. When we reflect on these losses, we cannot but feel that there has been a great want of practical humanity and caution in not providing more efficient means for saving life.

The loss of the Birkenhead iron troop-ship near the Cape of Good Hope, some fifteen years ago, furnishes a beautiful illustration of the value of discipline in cases of sudden emergency.

The details have escaped my memory, but I remember very well the effect on my mind of the one fact, that after embarking the women and the aged and sick, there being, unfortunately, no means for temporarily floating all the soldiers, they were drawn up on the quarterdeck, as if for parade, and went down with the ship.

This wreck occurred by striking on a rock quite near to the land; the weather was not boisterous; the ship broke in two, engulfing a large number.

While writing on the subject of wrecks, I cannot but congratulate the passengers on board the steamer Providence, which vessel ran into a scow in Hell Gate a few days since. All escaped without injury, although it is said that "all the upper works were carried away," which, of course, must be an exaggeration of the typos.

I notice also the loss of the "Lac la Belle," propeller on Lake Michigan, on the 14th October. It appears that she had about twenty passengers, and thirty-two belonging to the vessel on board, making fifty-two souls, and that she had "two life-boats, a yawl and two small boats," enough, one would think, if of proper size, to carry all; but it appears that several persons, afraid to trust to the small boats, remained by the steamer, and are supposed to have been lost with her. It seems very odd that these should not have found sufficient floating material to sustain themselves a short time. The vessel sank early in the morning; the best evideuce we have that the weather was not very bad is found in the fact that all the boats landed or were picked up.

One account says: "During the forenoon a propeller with two smoke stacks passed quite near to us, but made no response to our signals, although I am confident they saw us."

I trust that the writer of the above was mistaken. It cannot be true that any one bearing the human form could have been so dead to all humanity. It must be kept in mind that a small boat may be passed at sea quite near and not seen, unless a good lookout be kept. If it can be proved that a steamer passed by a boat as stated, the responsible party should be sent to Marblehead and served as Ireson was!

"Ireson, for his hard heart,
Was tarred and feathered and rode in a cart."

One of the most successful rescues, effected by means of a small mortar at Nantucket, was in the case of the schooner Eveline Treat, in December, 1865. She was cast on shore on the south side during a gale, and filled in the surf; a line was got to her, and by means of this a larger rope, which being set up on the beach and kept clear of the crest of the waves by a crotch, was used to convey the crew to the shore by means of a hanging bowline and a seat attached to it, like a common swing seat. When the captain came along the rope the hauling line fouled, and he was arrested midway, and in great danger of being swept off, when a gallant young man named F. W. Ramsdell mounted the rope, laid his body on it, and thus balancing himself, worked his way off to the captain, cleared the line and assisted him to land. The feat was performed in presence of many spectators on the beach.

General Remarks on other Means for Saving Life.

In No. 81, Volume 8, of the "Journal of the National Life-Boat Institution" of England, there is a very interesting paper by Admiral Ryder regarding the utility of the naval hammock, as a means for saving life in the now too common event of the sudden loss of a ship by collision, capsizing or blowing up by torpedoes.

In alluding to this paper I shall make use of some of Admiral Ryder's facts and arguments, and offer such suggestions of my own, as may lead to a thorough ventilation of the subject.

I have long persisted in suggesting that men-of-war should be furnished with life-boats, and every convenient and practicable form of life-preserver; there is no valid reason why fighting men, who ship to be killed and drowned, should not be furnished at the cost of the government they serve with means for rescuing them from sudden death when such accidents occur, as we have lately witnessed in the cases of the Captain; the Amazon; a Russian frigate, sunk at midday, by accidentally ramming another vessel; a British man-of-war, the Bombay, lost off the English Bank, Rio de la Plata; our own steamer Oneida, on the coast of Japan, and many others, fresh in the memory of my readers. The paper alluded to relates principally to the value of the hammock as a safe, handy and cheap life-preserver; I shall therefore confine my suggestions mostly to this article of furniture.

Commander Bridge, of the Caledonia, at Malta, September, 1870, reports to Admiral Ryder the result of experiments, thus:—"A well lashed hammock containing only a bed and blanket supported for a few minutes seven naked men; for a considerable time four men, and would, I believe, have continued to do so for nearly an hour. The officers who witnessed the experiment were, with myself, astonished at the floating power of the hammock. The hammock was a new one, and consequently less pervious to water than an old one would have been."

Captain Wilmshurst, of the Valiant, made further experiments, by order of Admiral Ryder. He estimates the buoyant properties of a hammock, thus:—

"Weight of water displaced by a well lashed hammock, ...	138.24 lbs.
Weight of same with bed and blanket, when dry, ...	24.5
Buoyancy of dry hammock, ...	113.75

Length, 55½ inches; Diameter, rolled up, 9¼ inches; Volume, 2.16 cubic feet.

A weight of 6 lbs. attached to one end of this hammock sank it in five minutes. If the same weight were attached to the middle it would float much longer: or, by actual experiment, nine minutes.

By simply oiling the bed-ticking the hammock floated two and one-half hours, and would, no doubt, have supported a man for that time."

Captain Wilmshurst says that the horsehair bed supplied to the seamen of the Royal Navy is *charged to them* at 10*s.* 6*d.*, that beds stuffed with *cork shavings* can be supplied by wholesale at 5*s.*, and with cocoanut fibre 7*s.* 6*d.*; the latter would be less buoyant but more comfortable. He states that a bed 6 feet long, 4 feet wide and 4 inches thick, stuffed with cork shavings, weighs 20 lbs. This will support 80 lbs. of dead weight. A mattress stuffed with cork shavings costs in England less than half the cost of hair.

In conclusion the admiral writes: "I have been told by an officer of rank, who was on board the Bombay when she was burned, off Monte Video, that if it had occurred to them to stand by hammocks, before the men jumped overboard, all hands might have been saved. Many of the men were drowned while the overladen boats near by could contain no more; the boom (or stowed boats) could not be got out, because the falls were burned, and there was not time to make a raft, as all hands were employed in attempts to subdue the fire until they were ordered to leave the ship."

Without stopping to comment on this large loss of life, from a first-class man-of-war, in smooth water, let us discuss, carefully, the value of the hammock.

The British hammock, with horsehair bed and pillow, will sustain a man who has his wits about him "*a considerable time*," —long enough to save him if there be vessels near by. This bed costs Jack 10 shillings.

A hammock with mattress of cork shavings, 6 feet by 4 and 4 inches thick, would sustain two or three men indefinitely, *at half the cost.*

Nothing but red tape, after this, ought to prevent a sale of all the hair beds in the navy, and substituting cork shavings. But it may be said, and said truly, that the comfort and health of the men is of more importance than saving a few when rare accidents occur, therefore, stick to hair. And hammocks stowed in the nettings (if such things have not become obsolete since ironclads came into fashion,) filled with hair beds and blankets, keep out grape and musket balls, therefore, stick to hair.

Perhaps cork shavings may answer this purpose even better than hair. For my part, I cannot see that the health of the men could be impaired by sleeping on cork shavings, *in a hammock.* A thin cork bed put *on deck*, would be hard, and perhaps impair health in the long run. I would inquire why hair mattresses cannot be entirely dispensed with in men-of-war for the men?

Conceding that hammock nettings, grape-shot and musket balls are out of date, and that ironclads may carry all their hammocks in lockers on deck, ready for capsizing and sinking gracefully in the day time, or suddenly at night; I would suggest that, instead of a common hammock and hair bed, costing poor Jack altogether a pound sterling, at the least, the government should supply, as part of the outfit, a water-tight bag to stow the hammock in. Such a hammock would be ready for any emergency, and would be very healthy and comfortable, would be very compact, and amply sufficient in buoyancy to float a man. Of course, all this is supposing the weather to be suitable, or not cold enough to chill a man through in a short time; this is a contingency difficult to guard against by any floating power where the body is to be exposed to cold.

All I ask is that the mattress and pillow, whether of hair, cork shavings, cork dust or air reservoir, shall be well made and furnished by the country, and its condition well inspected; occasionally the hammocks should be piped up and every man made to go overboard; in this way a raft could be made capable of transporting stores and all hands.

All vessels of war should be provided with means to float the whole crew by their hammocks. The objection to this for exercise is that wetting the bedding with salt water will be very objectionable on a large scale, and unless it is done on a large scale, the exercise will not be worth much. My attention having been called to the subject, I tried a mattress filled with cork shavings with an excellent result, so far as buoyancy is concerned; but the difficulty of drying bed and blankets thoroughly, induced me to make a close woven cotton canvas bag, sufficiently large to contain the common hammock and cork mattress, when made up as usual. This bag being carefully made, with a double seam, and a strong line to tie the mouth, was found to float two thirty-two pound shot four hours, and one shot indefinitely, only dampening the hammock. This adds but little to the cost of a hammock and bed, and keeps it dry and clean in the nettings. The only practical disadvantage which occurs to me is the fact, that putting in the hammock after being lashed, adds to the time necessary to prepare for the sinking of the ship. Subsequent trial proved that a hammock with the usual hair mattress, blankets, etc., could be kept up twenty-four hours, with one thirty-two pound shot attached to it, then another was added and it continued to float and was still floating the next day when the report was made.

I have heard of a well drilled crew reefing topsails in three minutes,—with such a crew,—life being at stake,—two or three minutes ought to suffice to open their peepers, make up and bag their hammocks, and be ready to go overboard or to join them to spars and casks for making a raft that would carry all hands. We hear a good deal about the active exercises of housing masts, changing topmasts and sails, lowering boats and landing howitzers, but very little as to saving life, except a case of a man falling overboard occasionally. I think a little more time, more means should be given, and more interest should be felt in saving life. Men-of-war do not have life-boats, nor do they give much study to anything but the means for keeping the ship in trim and making her effective in defending the flag. The list of stores, it is true, contains perhaps twenty life-preservers, not good for much, and an effective life-buoy or two, to drop over and show a light; these are very well so far as they go, but they do not go far enough. *Every boat's crew should be provided with a life-belt to be kept in the boat.* Every man-of-war should have at least one monitor raft and a gun rigged for casting lines, and every boat should be provided with some extra buoyancy by cork. We are very well aware that a boat going off *armed* on an expedition has little room for life saving gear; in such cases, it can be omitted; killing being the rule, and saving life the exception; still, for all general purposes, something should be added to the equipment for extra buoyancy. Take the case of the loss of Admiral Bell, and his Lieutenant and 11 men of his boat's crew, off the bar of Oasaka, Japan, for instance. If he had been provided with life-belts all would probably have been saved; whereas, only three escaped by swimming. The three cylinder monitor raft can carry out easily the stream anchor of a first-class steamer, weighing perhaps 2,000 pounds, and get rid of it without danger. At present, the usual means for carrying out an anchor of that weight is by one of the large cutter's, hanging it under her; this draws considerable water, and offers great resistance to pulling to windward or against tide, and in towing off by other boats; whereas, a monitor raft, carrying an anchor of 2,000 or 4,000 pounds, can be towed off handily, and will draw less water than the steam launch.

Loss of the Captain.

The loss of the ironclad Captain offers a very strong comment on the want of means in vessels of war for saving life in sudden emergencies.

I quote at some length from the English *Nautical Magazine* for October, 1870 :—

Lord Warden, at sea, off Cape Finisterre,
Wednesday, September 7th, 1870.

Sir,—It has been my painful duty to forward by Her Majesty's steam vessel Psyche to Vigo the following telegram, transmitted to the Lords Commissioners of the Admiralty, reporting the sad loss of Her Majesty's ship Captain with all hands, viz.:

"Very much regret sending painful news. Captain must have foundered in the night. She was close to this ship at two this morning; sudden S.W. gale. Very heavy squalls. Daybreak, Captain missing. This afternoon her boats and spars found. Crew unfortunately perished. Inconstant sails to-morrow morning with report."

I beg leave to transmit to their lordships full and early details of this most disastrous event. Yesterday morning, the 6th instant, I went on board to inspect the Captain, with Captain Brandreth and my flag lieutenant, and visited most minutely every part of her. At one P. M. a trial of sailing with the ships of the squadron was commenced and continued until five o'clock, when the recall was made. The direction of the wind was S. by W. Force about six knots—some of the ships carrying their royals during the whole time, Captain included. At six o'clock the breeze had freshened, and the speed of the Captain, which at first was nine and a half knots, increased to an average from eleven knots to thirteen knots. The sea was washing over the lee side of her deck, as she had a swell on her lee bow, the lee gunwale of deck being level with the water. I returned to the Lord Warden at half-past five P. M.

Being close to the rendezvous (twenty miles west of Cape Finisterre,) the squadron was again formed with eight divisions—the Lord Warden, Minotaur and Agincourt, Agincourt leading, the Captain being next astern of the Lord Warden. The signal was also made to take in two reefs and send down the royal yards, and the ships stood to the west-north-west under double reefed topsails, foretopmast staysail, and foresail topgallant sails furled, steam ready to be used as required, force of the wind about six to seven.

At eight and ten P. M. the ships were in station, and there was no indications of a heavy gale, although it looked cloudy to the westward. At eleven the breeze began to freshen, with rain. Towards midnight the barometer had fallen and the wind increased, which rendered it necessary to reef, but before one A. M. the gale had set in at south-west; our square sails were furled. At the time the Captain was astern of this ship, apparently closing under steam.

The signal "Open order" was made, and at once answered, and at a quarter-past one A. M. she was on the Lord Warden's starboard or lee quarter, about six points abaft the beam.

From that time till about half-past one A. M. I constantly watched the ship; her topsails were right close reefed, or on the cap; her foresail was close up (the mainsail having been furled at half-past five P. M.,) but I could not see any fore and aft sail set. She was heeling over a good deal to starboard. Her red bow light was all this time clearly seen. Some minutes after I again looked for her light, but it was thick with rain, and the light was no longer visible. The squalls of wind and rain were very heavy, and the Lord Warden was kept by the aid of the screw and after trysails with her bow to a heavy cross sea, and at times it was thought that the sea would have broken over her gangways.

At a quarter-past two A. M. (the 7th instant,) the gale had somewhat subsided, and the wind went round to the northwest, but without any squall; in fact, the weather moderated, the heavy bank of clouds had passed to the eastward, and the stars came out clear and bright; the moon, which had given considerable light, was setting. No large ship was seen near us where the Captain had been last observed, although the lights of some were partly, at a distance.

When day broke the squadron was somewhat scattered, and only ten ships instead of eleven could be discerned, the Captain being the missing one. We bore up for the rendezvous, thinking she might have gone in that direction, but no large vessel being in sight from the masthead, I became alarmed for her safety, because, if disabled, she ought to have been within sight, and if not disabled, in company with the squadron, and I signalled the following ships to proceed in the direction indicated, to look out:—Agincourt, to the southwest; Monarch, south; Warrior, S.E.S.; Inconstant, S.E.; Hercules, S.S.E.; Northumberland, east; Bristol, N.E.; Bellerophon, to the north by east; Minotaur also went N.E. These vessels proceeded about ten to eleven miles, but nothing was seen of the missing ship.

The greater part of the ships were recalled and formed in line abreast, and steered at three or four cables apart to the southeast, looking for any wreck. The Monarch first picked up a topgallant-yard of the Captain, the Lord Warden another with sails bent. Then some studding-sail booms, and on the Psyche joining me from Vigo at sunset, she reported having passed two cutters painted white, bottom up, with a large amount of wreck, apparently the hurricane deck, amongst which was found the body of a seaman, with "Rose" marked on his flannel.

I have thus stated all that occurred under the eyes of the flag-captain and myself, and I much regret to say, that I can come to no other conclusion than that the Captain foundered with all hands on board, probably in one of the heavy squalls between 1.30 and 2.15 A. M. of this morning, (7th instant,) at which time a heavy cross sea was running; but how the catastrophe occurred will probably never be known. I had the most perfect confidence in Captain Burgoyne, Commander Sheepshanks, and the executive officers with whom I had come in contact. Captain Burgoyne himself was a thoroughly practical seaman, and it is impossible that the Captain could have been better commanded. The service will mourn the loss of an officer of much ability and promise. I regret, also, Captain Coles should have shared the same fate. He had been several passages in his newly-constructed ship, and took a deep interest in all that concerned her.

I greatly deplore the sad event, which has cast a deep gloom on the whole squadron. I have, &c.,

(Signed) A. W. MILNE, Admiral.

Minotaur lost sight of Captain about 1.45 A. M.

Northumberland last saw Captain between nine and ten P. M., before the heavy rain set in.

Agincourt saw Captain last about eleven P. M.

Inconstant saw Captain last about 10.15 P. M.

Warrior saw Captain last about 10.30 P. M.

Bristol saw Captain last about ten P. M.

Psyche picked up one dead body and passed two cutters bottom up, and several other spars.

Monarch picked up main topgallant-yard and topgallant studding boom sail.

Bellerophon picked up bow roller of boom boat, white boat, a launch and six-oared boat.

Agincourt picked up part of cutter, two signal lockers, upper deck hatchway, broken gaff and topmast, deck planks, oars and mahogany office fittings.

Minotaur picked up two launch's oars, pinnace's sail in cover, and ensign.

Inconstant—Two oars and mahogany board and hammock netting.

Warrior picked up skylight, port, and small gear of turret and cabin-windows, sashes and pieces of inside lining.

Bristol picked up two oars, second cutter's breakers and two pieces of hammock netting.

Hercules picked up two swinging booms, jib-booms, three middling sail booms, all marked "Captain;" royal yards, standard, compass, splinted oars and part of a boat's upper deck grating; and half of bowsprit, with sword-belt, and handkerchief entangled.

Lord Warden—Mizen topgallant-yard, with sail bent, and office-desk and portion of small grating.

The Captain had a complement of more than 500 officers and men. Captain Cowper Coles, the designer of this ship, was on board, and has been lost. Mr. Childers has lost a son, so has Lord Northbrook. Sir Baldwin Walker has not only lost a son-in-law in Captain Burgoyne, but has to bewail the death of a son, who had gone on a cruise with his relative as an amateur.

Extracts from the *Western Morning News.* This tells us that—

All went well up to the 6th of September, on the afternoon of which day Admiral Milne and his staff went on board the Captain to witness from her a trial of sailing, in which she was to take part, with the Monarch, Inconstant and Bristol. The gallant admiral remained on board the vessel until the evening, happily declining the invitation of the officers to remain to dinner, and go on board his own ship next morning. When he left the Captain, at about 7 P. M., the sea was pouring over her upper deck in cataracts, so much so that the admiral's galley was nearly swamped whilst alongside. It is reported that when he arrived on board the Lord Warden, Admiral Milne was heard to say, "Thank God! he was on board his own ship again."

At seven o'clock the Captain communicated with the fleet by signal, and this was the last time she ever did so, as night soon after closed in. About this time a gale sprung up from the S.W., which all the vessels weathered out up to 1.30 on the morning of the 7th. At that time the Captain was seen from the Lord Warden steering N.N.W., under treble-reefed fore and main-topsails and foretopmast staysail. Fourteen minutes after, at 1.44 A. M., a sudden tremendous squall struck the fleet, the wind having shifted round to N.N.W. Nearly all the vessels were "taken aback," and a signal was made from the Lord Warden to "wear ships." The squall lasted for two hours, causing considerable loss to all the ships in the topsails, which were split and blown away. When the day dawned all the vessels of the fleet were in sight with the exception of the Captain. It was then presumed that when the wind shifted and the signal to "wear" was given she had not observed it, and standing on, was now out of sight.

Two theories were advanced in the fleet to account for the calamity. One, supported by Sir Alexander Milne, is that when the wind shifted at 1.44 on the morning of the 7th, the Captain was taken aback, and one sea swept over her; that before she had time to "shake herself free" from it another dashed on her, sweeping away all her upper works and her poop—which, by the way, from its shape, had been called "the coffin"—and that she then filled immediately and sunk. The other opinion is, and that is agreed in by many officers of great experience in the fleet, that when "aback" the sea burst in her large stern port—which was much larger than that in any other ship—and that she went down stern foremost. The manner of her loss will only be known when the survivors, who have been landed near Corunna, are able to tell the tale. It is evident that her destruction came upon her with fearful suddenness. Though in the midst of a large fleet she had not time to fire a rocket or make any signal of distress. Her boats, with the exception of her steam pinnace, a life-boat, which has since arrived with the eighteen survivors at Corcubion—were picked up at sea by ships of the fleet.

The *Hampshire Telegraph* publishes the following further details of the loss:—

Captain Burgoyne was on deck at the time when the accident occurred. He was dressed in his uniform cap, pilot cloth reefer, and an old pair of trousers. The ship was under steam and sail, with her double-reefed fore and main topsail, fore staysail, and the fore top-mast staysail set.

When the middle watch was called at twelve o'clock the weather was exceedingly squally, and the captain remained on deck giving orders. At five minutes past twelve the watch was piped to muster, and two minutes afterwards the men, with the exception of the marines, were on deck, and those who had been relieved were below in the act of turning in. As soon as the new watch were on deck, and before their eyes were perfectly open, the captain gave orders to man the weather foretopsail brace, and then to let go topsail halyards and lee topsail sheets. Subsequently the order was given to let go the weather topsail sheets. No sooner had the latter order been given, and ere it could be executed, a terrific sea struck the ship on the weather beam and swamped her decks. The men of the watch, with the captain, were now in the water, the ship being over on her side, and trembling violently in the endeavor to right herself. As soon as the men could see what was going on around them, the ship was floating with her keel uppermost, and nothing could be heard of the crew.

They were now fighting for life with the sea, and after about ten minutes or a quarter of an hour had elapsed, one of the party saw the ship's steam pinnace life-boat some yards off keel upwards. They then swam with considerable difficulty to the pinnace, the captain, Mr. May and an able seaman named Heard reaching it together. Heard had held on the captain by the collar of his jacket. With assistance, the captain succeeded in getting on to the pinnace with the rest of the party, and caught sight of a ship not a great distance off, which they believed to be either the Bellerophon or the Lord Warden. At this time the Captain had disappeared altogether. Urged by the gallant captain, the men shouted as loud as they could, "Ship ahoy!" for a considerable time, but got no response. So frantic were their cries for help that the men became perfectly hoarse, and the majority lost their voices altogether for a time, and endeavored to prepare themselves for what they conceived to be their fate, namely, a watery grave with the rest of the unfortunate crew. All this time the pinnace was being tossed heavily, and the men were frequently washed from its keel into the mass of seething waters around them, but succeeded in getting on again, with what little assistance their fellow-sufferers were in a position to render them.

After being tossed about for some time in this way, the men saw the ship's second launch floating towards them with two men in, and raised feeble shouts to attract their attention. When the launch came to within a short distance of the pinnace Captain Burgoyne shouted out, "Hold to your oars, my men; hold to your oars," which order was, as far as possible, carried out, and the launch got close to the pinnace, the men leaping joyfully on board her. The sea frequently parted the two boats, and ere Captain Burgoyne and the noble seaman Heard, before referred to, could get from the pinnace, she was some little distance off. Heard stuck by the captain, who remained, sad looking, but calm, and as firm as if on board the ill-fated ship he had commanded. Heard took hold of him by the hand and said, "Come, sir, let's jump!" to which he replied, "Save your own life, my man." Finding that the distance between the launch and the pinnace was rapidly increasing, the seaman said, "Will you come or not, sir?" when the captain replied, "Jump and save yourself. I shall not forget you some day." The seaman jumped, and with difficulty reached the launch, and was hauled on board, and within a few minutes the pinnace and the captain was lost sight of.

We turn now from all this sad detail to ask why so unprecedented an occurrence should take place as that a ship capsized should *turn over*, so that her keel should actually be uppermost; and while for two minutes in that position, she should actually sink stern foremost? It is an occurrence of which we have never before heard. And we naturally enquire, are the rest of our iron ships safe? Would not the same thing occur with them all? It would be well if we could assure ourselves that they would not follow the example of the Captain. Where was the centre of gravity of the unfortunate Captain? She herself furnishes the reply: it was so near to her upper deck, her turrets with their guns, that they turn her keel, the lightest part of her uppermost,—even out of the water. It seems unprecedented. And yet the Captain has been repeatedly under trial, reported on, considered to be perfection. And yet, after all, a mere gale of wind brings out this stupendous, this most alarming fact. She gets beyond her bearings, she turns over, so as literally to bring her with her *keel uppermost.* She "trembles violently" after being struck by a sea "in the endeavor to right herself," and she is not more than two minutes in that dreadful position before she sinks stern foremost. Such an event we believe to be without precedent. But we do trust that all future contract-built ships will undergo the test of their centres of gravity being found with all their weights on board when ready for sea. A court-martial or of enquiry, we are informed, as usual on all such occasions, is to take place; when it is possible it may appear why the unfortunate Captain should have shown her keel before she foundered.

Among the means for making the highways of the ocean more safe, may be cited the letter of M. F. Maury, Superintendent of the National Observatory, dated February 15, 1855, to some of the merchants and underwriters of Boston, on the subject of different routes for Atlantic steamers out and home. Nothing coming from the prolific pen of Maury strikes me as of more importance to the safety of Atlantic navigation.

The letter alluded to, with a chart and diagram, was published by the Board of Underwriters of New York, A. B. Neilson, then President. At that time we had a steamer, perhaps, once in ten days going and coming; now we have one *about every eight hours,* not counting those going to and from Canada in summer and Portland in winter.

Measures are being taken to induce the Board of Underwriters to republish the letter and illustrations alluded to, but in the meantime I shall quote largely from the letter of Lieut. Maury.

He says: "Illustrative of the lanes, observations of not less than 46,000 days were made on the weather, currents, etc.; I find the adoption of the lanes will shorten the passage to the west, and not increase the average east more than a few hours, if at all.

"While the time will not be prolonged, the danger of collisions will be materially reduced.

"The part of the route between the meridians 15° and 65° West, is from 150 to 300 miles broad, consequently there is a breadth of 300 miles where sailing vessels are liable to be brought into collision with steamers. Now, suppose we lay off a lane 25 miles broad near the northern edge of this space and another near the southern edge, and recommend the steamers coming west to use the former, and those going east to take the other; would it not contribute to the general safety?

"If these lanes be adopted and engraved on the charts, as on the one herewith, sailing vessels would take care to avoid them at night or in thick weather.

"The lane coming west is a better track than the one now used, and for these reasons: it is thirty miles shorter; it runs so far south of Cape Race and the

Virgin Rocks that no time need be lost in avoiding these in foggy weather.

"*In fact*, the nearer we go to Cape Race the shorter the distance by great circle; but *in practice*, the time is shortened by avoiding Cape Race.

"The shortest distance between Liverpool and Sandy Hook is 3009 miles, the average actually made is 3069, and the distance by the lane *coming* is 3038. By this route there is some favorable current along the northern edge of the Gulf Stream. The help thus gained gives the actual distance 2998 miles, or allowing a little for detour, 3018."

Speaking of the route out, Maury goes on to say:—

"Though the distance is greater by a few miles, yet on account of the Gulf Stream it is *in time* the shortest a steamer can take. It is 106 miles greater from Sandy Hook to Liverpool than by the home track, but the current will make up the difference, and the weather is more favorable."

As evidence in regard to the weather, Maury cites the result of a vast number of observations derived from logs, and seems to find therein ample proof that there is less fog and more favorable gales than further north.

He winds up by stating that one "lane" shortens the distance from Cape Clear to Sandy Hook and the Delaware 30 miles, while the other lengthens it 75 miles; but when measured for *safety*, and *in time*, it will prove the shortest.

With the chart before one the tracks appear perfectly practical, and, I think, ought to be followed; not as Maury suggests, principally to make sailing vessels safer, but to avoid the danger of collisions by steamers.

A word or two more on the new gun of Delvigne, and mode of charging:—

In October, 1869, I received a letter from this gentleman, from which I extract:

"The octogonal flèche is much easier to make true by a plane. I beg you to pay particular attention to my principle, namely, shortness of the barrel, smallness of calibre, giving thickness of metal and great strength, compared to the longer barrel and larger bore. There is no doubt my mode of loading with the touch-hole coming into the forward end of the cartridge, and the empty space behind it, gives considerable more power. My little gun, 20 kilos. weight, gives much more power than the blunderbuss of the same weight, and permits using a greater charge, carrying a heavier flèche and line, but to what degree we know not yet. Another interesting question of economy is to decide whether we can get necessary strength by cast-iron instead of brass, without increasing the weight too much; this question will be settled by experiments to be made in Belgium, where the foundries are open to all."

Again, on the 24th February, 1870, Delvigne writes in regard to the apparatus sent to the Humane Society:

"The block for mounting the gun may be made of any convenient form to stand the recoil, and the gun can be placed on it so as readily to be removed and planted in the soil when required. You will be surprised to see one vent at the extreme inner end of the bore as well as one near the forward end of the cartridge. The reason is this: Suppose the want of caps, or damage to the caps, intended to fire in the usual way at the forward end of the cartridge, you can put in powder in the rear vent and fire the charge thus. After putting in the paper cylinder to make the empty space behind the cartridge, 50 grammes of powder brings the forward end thereof to the forward vent. Your experiments must depend on the strength of your powder; it will be well to begin with 40 grammes. Forged iron or steel would be good for the guns, but would cost nearly as much."

The advocates of the French system lay great stress on the adaptability of the fléche to any gun on board of ships. A ship-carpenter can make a suitable projectile out of a hand-spike in ten minutes, and this can be fired from a boat howitzer or swivel like any other projectile, and may be made to carry a deep-sea line 100 fathoms. Many cases occur in manœuvring at sea, picking up wrecks or boats in a strong tide-way, or getting a hawser to a vessel to tow her, where the French "Porte Ammares" would be very useful.

In the "Annales du Sauvetage Maritime" of August, 1872, I find that Mons. Delvigne has been carrying on further experiments under the auspices of the government; from the report I gather the following facts:—

That the new gun of 20 kilos. throws out 300 metres of line, 8 millimetres in diameter, attached to a fléche of wood 8 kilos.; while the Perrier, or heavy long swivel, throws out only 250 attached to a fléche of 5 kilos. the line being 5 millimetres. For firing against a strong wind the fléche used is iron. In 1870, Delvigne experimented with a shoulder-arm weighing 10 kilos. out of which he fired a fléche of 400 grammes, being eight times the weight of the ball thrown by the mousketon, or "fusil de rampart," the charge being 10 grammes of powder, without any difficulty from the shoulder. In the Annales alluded to the question of adopting the fléche for ordinary uses is discussed at length. In 1870–'71, Delvigne passed eight months at Toulon, and for several days witnessed experiments on board of Admiral La Graviéres squadron. The carpenter was ordered to make a wooden flèche for a 4-pounder, which was quickly done. Here the experiments seem to have ended, it being assumed, apparently, that if a gun and a flèche and a line existed, nothing more was required!

Kites, called by the French "cerf volants," or flying stags, have been occasionally utilized for saving life by carrying a line from the shore to a wreck, and the reverse. This machine seems to have been invented by Captain I. Brodie of the Royal Navy, in 1817. It consisted of a sort of parachute, or air-bag of light material open at one side, to be sent off from the masthead by the force of the wind.

In 1854, I find the idea practically carried out by Kane, who constructed a kite of the usual form, with a tail, to which was attached a little bag containing instructions; by these means he rescued the crew of a vessel stranded on the ice, they being inaccessible to him on the opposite side of an open channel. The machine was constructed and sent over in about one hour, its fall at the right time and place being regulated by a tripping-line attached to the head of the kite.

It would be very easy to communicate with the shore from a stranded vessel by such means, provided the wind was favorable. In the Annales for 1868, I find notice of a buoy to be dropped from a ship, by Admiral Exelmans, one feature of which I highly approve, and that is to have attached to it a line of 1000 yards, carried on a reel, which in revolving gives a general alarm. I suggest that all life-buoys fitted to be dropped from a vessel to save a man falling overboard, should have a pudding-bag or floating anchor to keep them from being carried by the wind and sea to leeward faster than a man can swim. Many lives have been lost for want of some means to arrest the speed of the life-buoy.

In looking back at the long list of wrecks, it may not be out of place to offer a few general remarks as to the mistakes made. After the disaster, while sitting quietly at home, it is not difficult to see these mistakes and to apply the remedy; nevertheless, the discussion of these may in the future be productive of good.

In the case of the steamer Central America, Captain W. L. Herndon, foundered at sea, in September, 1857, everything was done by the gallant captain and his officers that could be done to save the passengers and crew, amounting to 592, of whom 419 perished,—that is to say, from the time the gale began on the 11th, until the brig Marine came near, a period of about 30 hours, everything was done that good discipline and good seamanship could do to free the ship of water and get her head to wind. At about 2, P. M., on the 12th, the Marine rounded to under her lee, and was requested to lie by the steamer, then half full of water, all hands manfully pumping and bailing. The account before me, in the U. S. *Nautical Magazine* of January, 1858, Vol. 7, says:—

"We had originally five wooden life-boats and one metallic; one of the wooden ones had been washed away. As the gale had abated since 10, A. M., orders were given to lower the boats. Two were lowered successfully, one was stove; of the other two stowed on the upper deck, one was successfully launched, but the metallic (Francis) boat was caught under the guard and stove, and almost immediately sunk."

The three boats, under command of petty officers, then commenced to carry the women and children to the brig. They were lowered in by means of bowlines from the lee davits. By the time these boats had got to the brig the second time, she had *forged ahead and gone to leeward five miles.* Then some sail was made to cause the steamer to approach the brig. In the two trips the boats had been much damaged, one alongside the brig, so as to be useless, one other so as to leak badly and get nearly filled with water, and the third so much as to require constant bailing. By the time she got back to the steamer she was unfit to receive any beyond her crew, and some one hailed and ordered her to keep off. Darkness had now set in. About this time the second mate, Jas. Frazer, deposes that all hope of saving the ship was at an end, and at a quarter to eight bailing was discontinued. Shortly after she went down stern foremost. The engineer, saved, testified that the engines continued to work up to 1, P. M., on the 11th, when they stopped at times for want of steam, until between 4 and 5, when the water finally put out the fires. The donkey boiler continued to work the Worthington pumps until about 8, P. M., when they became choked until on the morning of the 12th, the donkey was again started, and worked well until, at 9, the water being 9 or 10 feet high in the engine-room, the fire was put out. The only resort after this was to continue bailing, in the hope of keeping the ship afloat until the transfer of the people could be effected. Captain Badger, a passenger, testified "that as the boats approached there was a rush for them, and it was apprehended they would be swamped. About two hours before the ship sank, a schooner ran down under the stern, but could render no assistance for want of boats. The lights of this vessel were seen far to leeward. Rockets were fired from the steamer, and then she went down! The devoted Herndon remained on the wheel-house, and went with her at 8 o'clock Saturday night. I was standing on the quarterdeck. The captain said he would not leave; I promised I would remain, and so did Frazer, the second mate. All at once she made a plunge, and with a shriek from the engulfed mass she disappeared, and five hundred souls were left on the bosom of the deep with no hope of succor. At 1.15, A. M., Sunday, the Norwegian bark Ellen came running before it, and she hove to under short sail. The task of rescuing the survivors was nobly commenced, and by 9, A. M., 49 had been picked up. Diligent search was made until noon, when we bore away for Norfolk, where we arrived on the 17th."

I repeat, that up to a certain time everything was done that human ingenuity and good order could devise to keep the ship afloat.

But when, at about 2, P. M., on the 12th, the brig came under the stern, it did not occur to the captain that the best thing to do was to get a hawser to the brig, and taking in all her sail but the maintop-sail aback, allow her to ride by the wreck as near as possible. If this had been done many more, if not all, would have been saved. Of course it will be said, and by experts, too, that in a tumbling sea, to get a communication by means of lines and finally a hawser, was a difficult process. I grant, that without preconcerted measures, care, forethought, it would have been very difficult, but if at the time the Marine was seen running down, due preparations had been made with lines, hawser and buoys, assisted by a boat, there would have been no appreciable difficulty in mooring the brig to the steamer within an hundred feet, and being close at hand, the boats, with their precious freight, could have been hauled back and forth by lines with the help of few men. So again when the schooner came within hail. Or if the steamer or the vessels had been provided with means for throwing a stout line 80 or 100 yards, communication might have been established and all hands saved. A schooner once made fast to a large steamer like the Central America could have been hauled up within 50 yards and received every one with little risk. So much for the Central America.

In a pamphlet published January, 1855, I gave my views at some length on the subject of ocean steam navigation, and particularly on the loss of the steamers Arctic by collision and the Amazon by fire. I now give extracts from this pamphlet:—

Ocean Steam Navigation.

The terrible fate of the arctic, and the loss of so many valuable lives, is a theme about which too much cannot be said at this juncture, while the public heart is bleeding.

This calamity must be discussed in all its bearings, and in doing this, something must necessarily be said which will inflict pain; but the wounds must be probed in order to ascertain their depth, and in order to suggest the means to guard against similar accidents.

I shall endeavor to discuss the subject with a practical eye, and as I have no prejudices to overcome, and no interests of a private nature to serve, I hope that what I shall say will be considered as impartial, and as emanating solely from a desire to contribute my mite to the preservation of human life and the mitigation of the sorrows of the sea.

After the loss of the Amazon by fire, early in the year 1852, or late in 1851, I addressed a letter to the Boston *Daily Advertiser*, dated 10th February, 1852, which was published, and also extensively forwarded by circular to all those who had any interest in steam navigation and packet-ships. The letter was no doubt extensively read and soon forgotton. This does not deter me from publishing anew the material portions which have a bearing upon the recent calamity:

"I have made several passages to and from England, and to and from China, and have had the good fortune to go and come in fine ships, well commanded and well manned, and in nearly all cases (certainly all on this side of the Isthmus of Suez) I have found the organization nearly perfect as regards the *ordinary* routine of duty, both in the duties of captain, officers, engineers and stewards; but I must say, that in all my travels by sea in steamers, *I have not sailed in one* where I consider the organization *complete* for cases of sudden alarm by collision, grounding or fire. While I entertain a personal regard for every captain, and with one or two exceptions, for all the officers I have had occasion to travel with, and while I accord to them full credit for the qualities which constitute good seamen and gentlemen, I feel that I should not be doing the subject justice did I not point out in plain terms wherein the custom, or habit, of the service has led them to neglect to prepare their boats and crews by stationing them and by occasionally exercising them, so that on a sudden alarm, real, or only for the purpose of exercise, the men would, at a given signal, instantly proceed to their stations, and be prepared for any emergency. The ordinary routine of a steamer may be neglected without serious accident, the watches may be relieved a few minutes too late or too early, and in the event of a want of order in the daily duty, no very serious consequences would *necessarily* arise, but in a sudden alarm, it is absolutely vital to have *organization*, *discipline*, to insure any approach to concert of action; what would become of the crew of a ship of war, consisting of several hundred men, without discipline in cases of emergency, and particularly in case of fire, that element most to be dreaded at sea?

"In case of any such alarm, the crew is usually called to 'quarters,' that is to say, every man goes to his place at the call of the bugle or the roll of the drum.

"In every well regulated steamer, every man should have a station for sudden emergencies, and he should be reminded by sounding the signal (after due notice to the passengers) occasionally, so as to make him familiar with his place.

"In several steamers I have sailed in, I have seen a 'quarter bill' posted up, where all hands, as well as the passengers, could see it, and in it the places of the men were designated, and particularly for the usual and ordinary duties of the ship. I have seen the crews of several ships mustered on Sunday, and examined as to their names, cleanliness, &c., but in all m experience I have never heard of a merchant steamer's crew being mustered for stations for fire, collision, or on a general alarm. * * * * * * * * *

"The organization should not only be complete as to the stations of the officers and crew, but the stewards and servants should have certain specific duties to perform, and there should *always* be some small casks of water, some canisters of provisions and other necessaries placed in some convenient locality, ready for such emergencies."

The general suggestions contained in this letter cannot be too often repeated. I would remark, in addition to what is therein said, that it is of paramount importance, in order to carry out a plan of organization, to have more petty officers, more trusty and well-tried seamen. These can only be secured in our Atlantic steamers by giving extraordinary encouragement to good men to remain by the ship. The excuses now are, and I regret to say that in American steamers and packet-ships they are valid to a certain degree, that "we cannot get men in these short voyages who will stay by us. We leave New York oftentimes with firemen and seamen whom we have never before seen, and whose names we do not know, and they scarcely know under what names they have shipped. By the time we get fairly at sea, and begin to think of getting matters into ship-shape order, we find ourselves on the other side. In fact, all our time and all our energy is expended in taking in and making sail, steering the ship, keeping a good look-out, cleaning ship, and the usual duties of the sea. We have no time to drill green hands, or seamen who are strangers to us, in matters relating to boats; we do no expect to run anybody down, and we really cannot undertake to neglect the daily routine of ship's duty for the purpose of drilling strangers for emergencies which may never happen."

These excuses are not unreasonable. The public demands that the steamship, aye, and the sailing packet, shall make the quickest possible run, deliver her freight in the best order ahead of all competitors, and this must be done by a physical power only brought together for the first time a week since, and wholly dependent on moral suasion for its government. With such elements as we have to deal with, I submit that this is asking too much. But let me not dwell too long on the existing evils. I must come to the remedies. It is sufficient to say, in regard to the speed of steamships in thick weather, that the public voice insists on speed, and I am ready to sustain this verdict for several reasons. At a high rate of speed the time of danger and the chances of collision and of damage by gales of wind are lessened; and last, not least, the danger to the steamship and her crowd of passengers, in case of meeting an obstruction, is not so great as at a slow pace,—she can be more readily controlled by the helm. These are among the principal reasons for going at full speed in fogs, when the wind is usually moderate.

Much blame was attributed to the Europa for going at full speed when she run down the Charles Bartlett, in 1849. For my part, I think our speed saved us who were on board; had the ship struck us where the Arctic was struck, the Europa would most probably have been where the Arctic now is, at the bottom of the sea, and there would have been very few from either ship to tell the tale! Much blame is attributed to Captain Luce for doing exactly what the *proprietors* of all the Atlantic steamers try to do, and boast of when done: namely, to make the shortest passage, to beat all competitors.

I say, then, "go ahead" when you know where you are, and sound frequently when you do not. Sometimes fogs prevail for days at a time, and in certain locations, where there is the most danger of coming in collision, even for weeks; suppose the Atlantic steamers and packet-ships should by common consent, or by force of law, determine that five or six knots must be the limit of speed in foggy weather, and that bells must be rung, and whistles blown and guns fired! What a splendid accumulation of dangers would be present! To my mind the dangers of the sea would be vastly increased.

But there are certainly some things to be done. A certain number of picked men should be kept in the steamship, at whatever cost, and they should be sufficient in number to steer the ship, to keep the look-out, and to have charge under the mates of the boats, pump-gear and life-saving apparatus. Each boat should have a regular crew, each man to know his place in the boat, each boat should have a set of oars and some spare oars, and be in all respects a *life-boat*, and she should be provided with a mast and sail, compass and lantern, water breaker and hand port fire, and in some convenient and well-known locality a supply of stores should be placed, marked and kept ready for each boat. It is not necessary to provide roast turkey and plum-pudding, nor chronometer and theodolites, but a small supply of imperishable provisions in canisters, ready for emergencies. Every steamer in the Atlantic trade should have at least two large life-boats thirty-two feet long and about eight feet beam, lined with cork and fitted with life-lines, india-rubber buckets for bailing, compass, port fires, water breakers and other apparatus. Besides, at least, six life-boats, capable of carrying at least forty persons, all large ocean steamers ought to be provided with half-a-dozen vulcanized india-rubber *pontoons*, say twenty to twenty-five feet long, and from eighteen inches to two feet in diameter. These pontoons, when collapsed and stowed away, would not occupy together more space than a small boat, and could always be kept on deck, ready to be inflated and formed into rafts, or be attached by lines passing under the boats, so that for an emergency like that of the Arctic, the boats could be increased in capacity, so as to *sustain*, if not accommodate, a hundred more passengers; these pontoons may be made of any required size, and would vastly increase the chances of saving lives.*

---

*Since the above was written, the Perry or Monitor raft has been brought into use, as already stated.

As to other means for the better preservation of life, there are many floats styled life-preservers. Very few of these contrivances are of much value to persons who are panic-stricken. Metal cannisters of various forms have been got up. The most valuable of these floats is the invention of a Mr. Fitch, and is made by W. O. Haskell, Boston. Having tried it in the water, I speak understandingly when I say that it is next to impossible for a person to drown in tolerably smooth water with one of these fixtures properly applied. The Tewksbury seats are also valuable, particularly when two or more are lashed together. In regard to these stools, I have seen a strong seaman nearly exhaust himself by attempting to get his body balanced upon it, while I am confident that I could sustain myself for hours with one of them, without exertion, provided the temperature of the elements was not too low. But the best of all these floats is an invention of a New York engineer, Mr. Thompson, which consists of a comfortable chair, which, when opened or expanded, makes a most desirable life-preserver. This seat should be put on board of all steamers and passenger ships, particularly on rivers and other narrow waters. It is more expensive than any of the life-preserver seats, but this should not prevent its general adoption.

The Cartes life-preserver is an English invention, and is a most valuable one; it consists of a circle or ring of cork shavings, covered by painted canvas large enough to go round the body under the arms, and having sufficient buoyancy to support a full-sized person.

All these body-floats require fastening to the body, and are often entirely useless on account of the want of a litlle coolness or tact in adjusting them. Whatever body-floats are used, every state-room should be supplied with drawings of them, and full directions for their use. True, the agony of life may be prolonged only for an hour, or less, and life *cannot be insured* by any life-preserver; but in a case like the Arctic, many might have been saved, especially if the boats had been in sufficient number hovering about when the ship finally sank. While on the subject of floats and life-preservers, I would strongly recommend that every state-room door on board of steamships and river and lake boats, or others carrying large numbers of passengers, should be hung on "pintles and gudgeons," and have for a centre panel a metal box, three or four feet long by one or two feet wide, and about two inches thick, so that, in the event of a sudden fire, they would serve to prolong life until assistance could be rendered. Many, many lives have been lost, in my short day, for want of means to support life for an hour or less.

Various methods are in use for safely and quickly lowering boats. The most simple one is to have a strong pennant at each end of the boat, which by passing over a cleat on the davits, sustains the boat when once hoisted up by the tackles, which are then unhooked. When the boat is to be lowered, it is done by the pennants, which may be both suddenly let go, releasing the boat from the ship, or the after one may be let go and the forward one may be used as a painter. These pennants must be long enough to permit the boat to reach the water, and strong enough to sustain her. The usual difficulty is in clearing boats from the tackles simultaneously, and it often happens that the bow tackle is unhooked, and the stern tackle fouled by the boat swinging round.

Having said enough on the subject of floats and what are called "life-preservers," I come now to speak of other means tending to avoid collisions on the ocean during foggy weather and dark nights. There is a great diversity of opinion among nautical men of experience as to the propriety of making night hideous to the passengers by sounding the bell, blowing horns, firing guns and shrieking through the steam whistle; some contend that perfect silence is the best thing for *self*, and there is no reason why self should not be cared for first in this particular; for my part, I think that the steam whistle, systematically and regularly blown during fogs and thick dark nights is the safest and best thing; but in order to make it effective in ocean steamers, there should be a rule that one blast at intervals of five or ten minutes should denote a westerly course, two blasts an easterly course, and three blasts a southerly, and four a northerly course. This would be simple enough for Atlantic navigation, as Atlantic steamers in given localities are not beating about on diverse courses, like sailing ships.

There are so many steamers now crossing the Atlantic, going out and coming back *by the same track*, that the danger of collisions is much increased, though still very small indeed. To avoid this particular danger in some degree, I suggest that a rule be adopted for outward steamers habitually to keep a little more to the north or to the south than homeward bound steamers, after passing Cape Race. If a rule should be established to this effect by the regular lines, the chances of collision would be still smaller, and the sailing ships would generally be aware, when she heard the steamer's whistle in a fog, which way she was heading, not only by the number of blasts, but by the position or place of the ship.

A port fire or blue light burned at stated periods in thick weather finds some advocates, but it has serious disadvantages; it cannot be seen far in a fog, and it cannot denote the course of the ship, while it blinds the men on the lookout on board of the ship, and it would cost more than a little waste of steam. The steam whistle, then, I consider the true thing to warn an approaching ship.

One great cause of loss of life on the occasion of the loss of steamer Atlantic, on Lake Erie, and in the case of the Arctic, was, no doubt, the prevailing idea that sinking ships go down suddenly, creating a whirlpool or vortex. A sinking ship is, thank Heaven, not a usual sight, but it is not altogether a novelty with me, for I have been on board of one that capsized and sunk in a few minutes, and I have seen another sink under the bows of the Europa, and I am not a believer in jumping into real danger in order to avoid an imaginary one! Ships go down more or less suddenly, no doubt, and there is in some cases a tendency to draw down to a certain extent all those who may be on the deck, but not to an extent greater than would be the case by jumping from the ship's rail, in which process any ordinary "life-preserver" is likely to be damaged by breaking its fastenings.

This is a good occasion to illustrate the value of a good lookout from aloft several times a day, on board of all vessels at sea. There is no knowing how many despairing souls might have been saved, as was Captain Luce, by a good lookout from aloft, if every shipmaster should send a man aloft several times a day, to look for wrecks, particularly in the stormy Atlantic.

I have treated of the means obviously useful for saving life in cases of sudden wreck, and I come now to make some suggestions as to more extensive means for this great end in steamships. All steamers, whether of wood or of iron, should have a practically water-tight bulkhead before the engine-room, and another abaft the same, so that any serious fracture at either end would enable the engines still to work, and keep the small leaks under. True, the bulkhead cannot be always perfectly tight, but we must not give them up for this reason, any more than we should give up ships because they sometimes leak.

The saloon-deck of steamers, generally sixty or eighty feet long, may be so built and fastened to the standing part or sides as to be detached at short notice and form a valuable raft, especially if spars, pontoons and life-lines and railings are so prepared as to meet the exigency. A short time ago, the idea of constructing a steamer so as to sink with comparative safety to her passengers, would have been met with ridicule; but we now realize, from the sad experience of the Arctic, that good ships can sink, and that many lives can be lost by sudden accidents for want of precautions in their original construction. Besides the saloon-deck and the bulkheads, it would be a good plan in constructing sea steamers, to have all hatches, doors in bulkheads and other apertures, so contrived that they can be closely fastened; firstly, to exclude air in cases of fire, and next, to keep in the air when the ship is, by an accident like that to the Arctic, gradually sinking. I do not hesitate to say, that had the engines of the Arctic been stopped as soon as the probability of sinking was imminent, and all the ports, dead-lights and hatches securely caulked and fastened down, the ship would have filled much less rapidly; it is not necessary that the apertures should be entirely air-tight, nor that the bulkheads should be perfectly water-tight in order to *stop the vent.* As fire on board ship is not uncommon, we all resort in such a case to *excluding the air*, and I see no valid reason why we should not *keep the air in* when the leaks get the better of the pumps.

I come now to speak of the mistakes made in the management of the Arctic. In making these remarks, I would not be understood as implying blame to the gallant commander. From a personal knowledge of him, I am quite sure that he thought only of the safety of his passengers, and while I make some comments on his proceedings, I would frankly say that it is much easier, while sitting by our firesides, after the disaster, to suggest what ought to have been done. It was a fatal mistake to run the ship when it was ascertained that the leak was rapidly gaining on the pumps. The land was forty or fifty miles distant, and every revolution of the wheels not only increased the leak, but carried the ship further from the direct track of vessels. The ship should have been arrested in her course, and all the means applied to getting the boats safely manned, all apertures should have been carefully closed, and the masts should have been cut away, as they would have done more towards forming rafts than all the spare spars. In all the accounts which I have seen, not one word is said as to any attempt to cut away the masts; perhaps no axes were at hand, and if this is true, it shows a lamentable want of precaution for an emergency liable to happen to any ship. Allowing that the officers and most of the crew had already accidentally or wilfully left the ship, it can hardly be possible that there were no passengers who could handle an axe, and the only way that I can account for the omission of this expedient, is by supposing that the axes had been taken away, or that the ship was not provided with them. But the great cause of the immense loss of life was the want of due organization for such an emergency, and this cause operated to a fearful extent in consequence of the want of sufficient boats to take anything like the whole number of persons comprising the crew and passengers of the ship.

Great allowances must be made for Captain Luce, when we cast any imputation on his judgment in running the ship after he was sure that nothing could save her. Who is there with such a vast accumulation of responsibility on his mind and heart who would have done more than he? Surrounded as he was by despairing friends, looking to him for superhuman exertions, practically deserted by his men and by most of those to whom they had been accustomed to look up to for orders and control, what more could he do than to raise his voice, and by his manly example show that if he had been properly supported many might have been saved. As to the desertion of the firemen and seamen, little more need be said than that they obeyed the instinct of self-preservation. They are not usually men from whom you would expect a different course. With few exceptions, they were men without any particular attachment to the ship, or to her officers or passengers. If they had been duly organized for such a fearful crisis, and if they had felt that the boat would contain every soul on board, there would have been put on the record of humanity many acts of disinterestedness and devotion to duty. But without discipline, *preconcerted and duly enforced discipline*, what else could have been expected of them than to rush for the boats? The few who did not do this deserve to be enrolled among the heroes; but I doubt not there were among the deserters many men who, under proper control, would have equally deserved the name!

I understand from one of the survivors of the Arctic's officers, that she had a good set of seamen on high wages, and that they were generally sober men; men to be relied upon in time of danger from the ordinary perils of the sea. I can, if this be true, only attribute their anxiety to leave the ship to a want of confidence in the means provided for saving them. True, the law says that the seamen must stick by the ship and assist the passengers, and after seeing them safely deposited in the boats, they may sink or swim at their leisure, if there be no means to buoy them up. But what seaman, who has not served in a ship of war, under strict orders, and having a certain amount of "esprit du corps," can be expected to study the niceties of Blackstone or Story on board a sinking ship!

I *pity* the man who lost so good an opportunity of distinguishing himself, but I can scarcely *blame* him. Life in a coal-stained skin and a red shirt is as dear as if clad in broadcloth and velvet.

Finally, the ceiling and timbers in the wake of a steamship's engine room should be closely fitted and made water-tight between the bulkheads. In this case a leak in the fore-hold, or after-hold, or in any place forward or abaft the bulkheads, would be kept from flooding the engine-room; and the pumps, even those attached to the engine, could be worked much more effectually than when in danger of being flooded.

In the case of the loss of the Amazon, by fire, 1851 or '52, the engineers were driven from the engine-room, and there being no means for stopping the ship accessible from the deck, she ran at speed, and in the attempt to lower the boats, they were swamped, and many lives were lost. Having no account at hand I am unable to state how many were rescued, or by what means.

This is a good place to reiterate what I have often said, namely, that every steamer should have means for shutting off steam from the deck, and donkey boilers and engines, for pumping and throwing water, should be located, not as usual, in some corner of the engine-room, but in some place much more accessible from the upper deck.

Many cases could be cited besides the Amazon, the Central America, and the America, to show the folly of placing the donkey engine and boiler, in or near the engine-room.

The recent loss of the Pacific Mail Steamer, by fire, in the Harbor of Yokohama, so well detailed in the *Daily Advertiser*, of the 12th Oct., shows the necessity for keeping up steam in the donkey boiler at all times, when the main engines are not in use. The want of steam seems to have been the principal cause of the loss of this noble ship, and so many lives. Next to this the preparation of the boats and rafts, was too long neglected in the necessity for fighting the fire. To one looking at the loss of this fine ship, from this side of the Continent, it seems inexplicable that so many lives should have been lost, in a smooth harbor, with plenty of vessels at hand, and I cannot but think that there was a great want of good management on the part of the spectators.

In the case of the Bienville, recently lost by fire, every one acquainted with Capt. Maury gives him credit for being a thorough seaman, and a humane gentleman; but here is a case where the resources provided by the owners in boats, floats, or rafts were insufficient for the emergency, and some of the means provided, were of an unstable character.

Not having seen any detailed account of the examination of Capt. Maury and his officers, or of the survivors. I abstain from making any extended comments on the loss of this ship, and part of her people.

In the case of propeller Metis, recently lost between Watch Hill and Point Judith, I would remark that I have seen no official report of the examination by the inspectors; but I have read all the newspaper details, and I do not remember to have seen or heard a single word on what appears to me, to have been the great neglect or oversight; and that was, in not immediately bringing her wounded side to windward, and by every means giving her a list to starboard, in order to get at and stop the fracture. The wind being to the South or Southeast, blowing on shore pretty fresh; if her head had been put to seaward, her anchors let go, and exertions made to heel her to starboard, the chances are that the leak could have been kept under control by the full power of her steam pumps. Whereas, when too late, it was found that she was leaking badly, she was run at full speed towards the land, directly away from the well known track of passing vessels. In this case there was a lamentable want of organization; the boats were insufficient as life-boats, were under little control, and the metallic pontoon or raft, scarcely mentioned in the published accounts, appears never to have left the hurricane deck, until it broke up. I would much like to know, how much this raft did towards the saving of life, and how much it failed to do.

The loss of the Metis will be forever remembered as illustrating the great value of the detachable upper deck. Although it was not made to come off, it is quite clear that it was the means of saving many lives. If the steamer herself had reached the shore nearly full of water, drawing fifteen or twenty feet, and been thrown among the breakers, perhaps a quarter of a mile from the beach, the chances are that more lives would have been lost than by remaining where she was struck, even had she filled there and sunk, or by going down where she did. As a schooner's bowsprit is several feet above water, it is fair to conclude that the main fracture was mostly above water, and that if it had been properly examined and measures taken to stop the hole, instead of forcing in the water by keeping on, the result would have been very different.

To go back a little to ocean disasters, I would cite the case of the steamer Connaught, lost near our coast in October, 1860. She first sprung a bad leak and then took fire. The whole crew were saved by the brig Minnie Schiffer, Capt. Wilson, who got a hawser to the steamer, and thus quickly and safely rescued every soul. But for the close connection between the steamer and the brig, many lives would probably have been lost.

In the winter of 1865–'6, the ship Caledonia, with immigrants, became disabled in the Atlantic, not very far from our coast. All hands were rescued successfully by boats, by the bark Fredonia, Capt. Burke, whose management met the high encomiums of the Humane Society and of the public. He threw over a considerable part of his cargo to make room for the passengers and brought them into port. He did not make a connection between his vessel and the ship. Not knowing all the circumstances of wind and weather, and knowing that he saved all, the inference is that he acted for the best.

I have before me the report of the Chief of Revenue Marine, N. B. Devereux, for 1870, to the Secretary of the Treasury, on revenue cutters, hospitals and life-saving stations, from whieh I extract the following useful information, relating to the life-saving stations and means for saving life generally. At page 43, I notice that the credit due to Capt. Ottinger for the origin of the life-car is acknowledged. There are twenty-eight stations from Cape May to Sandy Hook, on the Jersey shore, and twenty-six between Coney Island and Montauk Point, on the Long Island shore. There is an interval of five miles between each station. Congress appropriated $15,000 to the Humane Society of Massachusetts in the year ending June 30, 1871, to be accounted for to the Secretary of the Treasury, and a further act provided for pay of six men to each alternate boat station, on the coast of New Jersey and Long Island, from 15th December to 15th March, at the rate of $40 per month. This pay is stated to give these men at the rate of more than double the compensation the keepers receive, which is $200 per annum. The report recommends correcting this, and giving keepers $350, and also increasing the salaries of the two superintendents, H. W. Sawyer and H. E. Hunting, to $2,000 per annum; also that the crew be paid a regular salary. The report treats fully on the various boats used and recommended for use on the coasts of New Jersey and Long Island, and alludes to the Manby mortar and the Delvigne processes. In speaking of the former, page 55, it says, "with a 5½ inch mortar and 14 pounds of powder,

Manby threw 310 yards of deep sea line, and with an 8 inch mortar nearly 479." Of course it was intended to say 14 ounces and not pounds. The report also says that the Delvigne process had not been conducted on a proper scale. To this I would say, that I have before me the most exhaustive trials of the process, under government authority. The report also says, that if Manby threw out, experimentally, 479 yards, there ought to be no difficulty in throwing out six or eight hundred. To this I would remark, that if we have a 15 inch mortar and a suitable charge, and a sufficiently strong attachment to a heavy projectile, we can throw a rope a mile or more. But this is not the question; the limit as to range must necessarily be governed by the ability to transport the mortar and its gear along a sandy shore. One very important consideration is suggested in this report, and this is to have scientific and elaborate tests made by U. S. Engineers, so as to provide the best means for throwing lines to wrecks.

Looking back a little, to a lecture given in 1867, for the benefit of the Snug Harbor, I find some hints worth repeating.

In allusion to the loss of the City of Bath, off Hatteras, under distressing circumstances, it was recommended that steamers be provided with means to inject steam into the coal-bunkers and cargo spaces, in order to put out fire; the pipes capable of being operated from the deck. Since that paper was printed I have heard of steamers so fitted, and I have recently noticed that the America, lately destroyed in Japan, had means for thus extinguishing fires; but she had not steam to spare, either to pump water or to put out fire, when lost. Donkey engines and boilers are generally used for washing decks and hoisting cargo, rather than for putting out fires!

Allusion was made in this lecture to the utility of pumps operated by hand, supplied by a suction hose, to be put over the side at any convenient point. One or two powerful pumps, thus fitted, would be valuable as auxiliary to the steam pumps, and might save life and property sometimes when the steam pumps give out. Reference is also made to a plan originating with Mr. Gray, of London, for making water-tight bulkheads in iron ships *double*, leaving a space of a few inches between them, so that the space could generally be kept full of water, as a preventive against fire. This plan would make the hull stronger, provided the bulkhead was properly put in and stayed.

Cargo hatches should be packed so as to be water-tight, and each compartment should have its steam pump connection, as well as hand pumps competent to keep the water within control, even if the bottom should be fractured, and provided the cargo itself is buoyant. Much may be done in the construction and fitting of ocean steamers *towards sinking very gradually* when stove by grounding or by collision. Even if the ship cannot be saved, she may be kept above water for hours, so as to afford a chance for rescuing the lives of her people. Many cases have occurred where the gain of an hour or two would have saved many lives. Such a gain as this, as I am assured by a practical engineer of great repute, may be attained by making the boilers of steamers subservient to keeping them afloat, for a time; that is to say, if the proper arrangements be made originally in the fitting of the boilers, and the right thing done in such cases as the Artic, Metis, and others, they can be converted into floating power instead of adding to the dead weights which tend to sink the ship.

Much has been said and much has been done in the way of invention and in the way of legislation, in regard to boat-lowering apparatus. Among practical men few of the patent arrangements find favor. Simultaneous lowering machines and detaching machines work very well on paper. So far as my experience goes, nothing is more simple and safe than the usual hoisting tackles, taking care, however, to *put the rings in the lower blocks and the hooks in the boat;* this renders the hooking on and unhooking of boats very much more safe. After hoisting up the boat thus, she should be hung by stout pennants, securely made fast inboard, and sufficiently strong to do the duty of a tackle, and long enough to permit of lowering the boat to the water, when they may be let go simultaneously; the after one thrown over and the forward one used as a painter. I believe that this mode of lowering boats will, in the long run, be found the simplest and best.

The usual contrivances for davits, or cranes for hoisting up boats, in merchant vessels and steamers generally, have descended to us from our forefathers, and should be modified in all places where the standing rigging does not interfere, by an arrangement adopted by me, whereby the boats may be hung inboard; or over the gunwale; or further out, ready to lower. The arrangement consists of two stout timbers or stanchions fastened to the side on a line with the rail or the edge of the hurricane-deck, and extending about four or five feet above the rail or deck, to these are attached two flat bar davits, eight or ten feet long, connected together by a spar swivelling on gudgeons at the head of the davits, to this spar the boat hangs. The guys which support the davits must be set up to the rail or deck in a true line with the bolts on which the foot of the davit swings out and in, and then the boat can be swung out and in with great ease, the motion of the davits being controlled and regulated by lines leading from their heads across the deck, and by a stout chain and tackle leading from the middle of the davit through an eye on the head of the stanchion. A ship's launch, or a heavy life-boat can be got in and out by this arrangement by few men, without the aid of stay or yard tackles. It is specially adapted to passenger vessels, which, going in and out of dock frequently, must as a rule, have their boats inboard, and ought to have them at all times ready to swing out. As now arranged the boats are stowed in chocks on deck, covered with canvas, fitted to be lowered only by considerable labor and after long delay. My arrangement will save full half the labor and time, whether it be three minutes or twenty.

The life-preservers required by law, must be sufficient in number for all hands, and of capacity to float sixteen pounds dead weight; this is little enough when it is considered that in a panic one will have often to do double duty. Wherever they are placed, there should be illustrations of the mode of attaching them.

Among the dangers to which iron vessels and steamers are exposed, whether of wood or iron, is the effect of local attraction on the needle, exposing them to great errors in their courses; by constant study and frequent observations of celestial objects vessels running in a given trade can and usually do get along tolerably well; they have a table of errors for every point of the compass to be applied on every course or to be registered or recorded on a distorted card by which the course is regulated.

The Savans of the Old World have not found any universal panacea or means for curing local attraction, so that a vessel corrected here or in London can navigate with the same corrections into the Southern Hemisphere. Many devices by means of magnets and soft iron have been tried, and some of them have done well in particular ships in particular trades; but no one that I am aware of in Europe pretends to correct local attraction for both hemispheres.

We have a man in this country who has corrected for me several iron vessels, where the compass was practically useless; in some cases more than *ten points* out. These vessels have gone to China, and to the Rio de la Plata, sailing by their regulated compasses, without any table of errors, entirely free from the effect of local attraction.

This is something that has neither been done or attempted in Europe.

No single thing will tend more directly to lessen the dangers of the sea than a reliable compass, speaking for itself, and not dependant for its integrity on a table of errors.

Among the small things requisite as helps to safety, I would suggest that every ship's boat be provided with a *pudding-bag drag*, a conical bag similar to the canvas log chip; having its cable, and its tripping-line for spilling or reversing it, this little machine will be found very useful to lay-to by, or to use in running through a surf. Another very important auxiliary to safety in laying-to, in scudding, and calming the waves when transshipping passengers, will be found in dropping over oil in small quantities; it has a wonderful effect in keeping the water from breaking; a good drag, and a keg of oil in a sea-way will make an ordinary boat comparitively safe.

In the education of youth, swimming should be taught as well as riding, or dancing, or skating, and generally will be found as useful as either in saving life and promoting health.

We find that in foreign countries the governments take a prominent part in encouraging life-saving associations, and although the principal associations are supported by voluntary subscriptions, the governments furnish valuable aid by the loan of materials, and by drilling their coast guard for saving life, as well as for saving revenue. If any new invention comes up it is fully tested by the government. It is to be hoped that our government will follow the example of England and France in this direction, and if it cannot give the aid of its coast guard, let it grant liberal sums for protecting our seaboard, and permit its revenue officers, and its ordinance officers and engineers to aid all humane efforts for saving life.

In May last, officers were detailed to examine and report on sundry life saving means, at Seabright. The board consisted of:—

J. H. Saville, *Chairman,*
Chief Clerk Treasury Department.
C. S. Boggs,
Rear Admiral.
C. B. Patterson,
Hydrographic Inspector of the Coast Survey.
William Gaskell,
Charles W. Maxson,
Experts in Surf-boats.

The report of these gentlemen, a copy of which I have before me, says: "the trials were conducted by Capt. John Faunce of the Revenue Marine. The wind was fresh from southward and eastward but with a very moderate sea, not enough surf to afford an approximately fair test of the qualities of the life-boats.

"The mortar charged with three ounces of powder, threw out 210 yards of line and with a larger charge would have gone farther; the committee wisely recommended the Government to make extended experiments with large mortars, and also to devise some better mode of attaching the line, or becket, to the shot. Next came an experiment with a rocket invented by Mr. Lilliendahl, 'consisting of a steel cased rocket with a long metallic loop to serve as a staff and an ingenious and simple way of attaching the line, the rocket is fired from a tube resting on a tripod arranged for any required elevation, the charge is ignited by a lock, the line running clear from a box.'

"At the first fire, the line parted in consequence of fouling a fence; the second and third trials gave highly satisfactory results, stretching out 283 yards of line against a fresh breeze."

The size of the line, and the angle of elevation are not given; another rocket contained in a paper case was tried but was not approved.

The Committee wisely recommended extended trials of the Lilliendahl rocket, so as to get a just medium in regard to cost, range, etc.

The first boats tried were three cedar boats, common to the location, and popular with the surf-men. They were presented by Messrs. Curtis, of Squam, Waddel, of Deal, and the Coast Wrecking Co., of Long Branch.

"They went off rapidly together in fine style and although the surf was only moderate, the manner in which they were launched, and handled evidenced their superior qualities as surf-boats, and gave promise of what they are capable of doing in a high surf, and bad weather."

The size, weight, and extra buoyancy of these boats, is not given; I presume they are mere shells, and have no extra buoyancy in the shape of air-cases or cork.

Next, the American Monitor Raft Co., presented one of their rafts, manned by seven men, "it was launched at the same moment with the boats, and gave evidence of possessing many good points as a life saving vehicle," this is all the report says as to the Monitor raft.

Next came the trial of the iron boat of Lieut. Stodder, the report says:

"A crew consisting of thirteen took their places in the boat, with tossed oars, and she was successfully launched from the wagon, the trucks of which were just within the edge of the surf. The impetus obtained in her descent on the inclined skids, shot her a full length into the surf, but it was only by a tremendous effort of the crew that she was kept head to the sea, until the full force of her oars could give her headway; when this was obtained however, she was rowed easily to seaward, floating with much buoyancy, displaying very excellent qualities, as also a handsome appearance on the water. In designing this boat, Lieut. Stodder has combined many of the best points of the boats in use on the coast of Great Britain, and has succeeded in producing a boat of fine model, amply buoyant, self-baling, and self-righting; but, in its present form larger than necessary, and in the opinion of competent judges, altogether too heavy for use, except at two or three points along our coast."

The Committee do not give the weight or size, or describe the means for self-righting and baling, nor do they say that these were tested. I infer, however, from what follows, that time did not admit of a more thorough trial. I have since learned through the press, that in a trial in Newport harbor, the self-righting and bailing qualities were successfully tested.

Next, the Beaupré life-boat was presented for trial. The Committee say:

"She was launched like the Stodder boat, is similar in general design, but very inferior in model, and did not impress the Committee favorably."

The Committee refer to a description of this boat by Messrs. Prindle & Co., from which I gather the following information. This communication was made to the Board, on the 3d of June, a week after the trial.

JOHN H. SAVILLE, ESQ.,
Chief Clerk Treasury Department:

DEAR SIR:

We have the honor to submit the following remarks with reference to Life-boats for use at the life saving stations upon the Atlantic coast, and request that they may be presented to the Board of Examination, of which you are the head.

The time allowed for building and presenting the Beaupré Life-boat was so short, as to render it impossible for us to obtain a correct understanding as to the especial features required for the service, and therefore, our boat while fully illustrating the principles involved, proved entirely unsuitable by reason of its excessive weight and defective model. Had a sufficient length of time been obtainable, in the latter respect at least, our boat would have been constructed in a satisfactory manner.

From the light now had upon the subject, we are of the opinion that the self-righting principle, however advantageous in the open water, is of little or no use in the surf, and that therefore, it should be dispensed with in boats intended for the purpose above named, by which means the weight and cost of the boat could be reduced nearly or quite one-third, and the improved device rendered far more easy to handle than would otherwise be possible.

The second principle involved in our boat, viz.:—Self-baling, is of vital importance to surf-boats, which as we are informed, are frequently filled by the surf one or more times before they can be launched in rough weather; such filling entirely destroying the usefulness of ordinary boats, and rendering it necessary that they should be baled out before a farther attempt at launching can be made. With our self-baling principle applied to a boat, the only effect produced by the shipping of water would be to temporarily increase the difficulty of propulsion, as by adapting the capacity of the lifting chambers to the weight to be carried, the water thus shipped can be caused to pass from the boat in ten seconds, leaving a margin of twenty seconds before a second wave would strike it, during which interval sufficient headway could be obtained to carry said boat beyond the point of danger.

While firmly believing that metallic boats are best adapted for the service required, we are of the opinion that some advantage may arise from the use of wood, and would state that the self-baling apparatus can be applied to such boats as readily as to those constructed of or from iron, and that when thus protected from swamping, surf-men would be enabled to go to sea in weather when no ordinary boat could live for a moment.*

While at Seabright, on the 27th ult., we conversed with nearly all of the surf-men present at the trial of life saving apparatus, and found that without exception they considered the self-baling or emptying principle of *great* importance, and that, if applied to their cedar boats, the greatest obstacle to a passage through the surf would be removed.

In view of the above, we propose to furnish for use at life saving stations, metal or wood boats, constructed upon any model required, and which, when filled, shall be capable of automatically relieving themselves from water, in from ten to fifteen seconds, when provided with a full working crew.

Very Respectfully,

PRINDLE & CO.

WASHINGTON, D. C., JUNE 3D, 1872.

---

*No light wooden boat could be built so as to insure keeping the air-case in the bottom tight.

The Commission say that they "did not have an opportunity to examine either the Stodder or the Beaupré boat in detail or critically. The time required for a thorough consideration of the subject could not be spared, and it is believed that a better and more satisfactory examination and report can be obtained by selecting persons who can avail themselves of more time, and at a season when the various appliances can be put to the test of actual use. From the limited examination we were able to make, we were convinced of the superiority of the cedar boats over any other for general service on the coast of New Jersey. That these boats have been found by the long experience of practical surf-men to be the best adapted for any sort of work in the surf, is sufficient argument in their favor, without more than a passing allusion to the fact that these men could never be induced to use any of the boats of different shape supplied to the stations since their first establishment. Therefore, we recommend that a boat of similar model be placed at every station. It appears, however, to be worthy of consideration whether these boats may not be improved by adding air-chambers and other appliances as will make them self-righting, without materially increasing their weight or changing their form. Also, whether they may not be constructed of galvanized iron, and thus provide against shrinkage and dry rot. To determine those points it is recommended that Captain Gaskill, an experienced surf-man, be authorized to propose plans, specifications and model of such a boat as in his judgment will be best adapted for ordinary service in all weathers on the New Jersey coast."

The Commission also recommend that Lieutenant Stodder's system be applied to smaller and lighter boats, and that a "number of these be placed at points adjacent to such inlets as may admit of the egress of the boat seaward with a crew of seven men."

The Commission speak of sending the boat-wagon and Stodder's boat to Narragansett pier, where I understand they are now located.

During the boat trials Mr. Meriam exhibited his life-preserving dress, which was very highly approved and recommended for the stations. Coston's night signals were also exhibited and approved of.

In conclusion the report says: "Our visit to Seabright convinced us that the life-saving service deserves the fostering care of the department, and in order to carry out the generous and humane designs of Congress the service should be thoroughly reorganized."

Everybody must heartily concur in these sentiments and in the suggestion to have more full trials of the boats and other apparatus.

BOSTON, 6th September, 1872.

ADMIRAL C. S. BOGGS, Washington.

Dear Sir,—I have read the report of the trial of life-boats, at Seabright, on the 27th May, with great interest, and concur with its general purport. I take note particularly of what is said on pages 7 and 8, in regard to the want of time and suitable weather for a thorough trial. Allow me to call your attention to an article furnished to the *Daily Advertiser*, on or about the 10th ultimo, wherein I advocate a more extended trial in more suitable weather, so that the several boats, the raft and rockets, can be tested more fully. After reading your report, I am more than ever convinced that this ought to be done before expending much money.

There should be *first* a boat of the approved New Jersey model, built of galvanized iron, to be furnished with air-tanks of considerable capacity, say 40 gallons, in the ends; cork floats on the outside, say 8 inches in diameter in the centre, tapering to 3 or 4 at the ends, and two cork floats on the inside under the thwarts, say 1 foot in diameter, fitted with beckets and capable of being removed at pleasure, to use as transporting buoys and for various obvious purposes as life saving material. The end tanks should be separate and distinct from the shell of the boat and not a part of it, so that they can be removed for examination, painting, etc. If on trial in competition with a simple cedar shell, this boat should be found too heavy to handle in launching, all the extra weight, such as tanks and floats, can be removed in a few minutes, so as to give her a fair chance; iron against wood in a rough surf.

So long as the wooden boat remains sound and free from water, she will compete successfully with all others—but the moment a fracture takes place, opening a leak, or a sea breaks on board, it is clear that the boat provided with floats will sustain her crew and others, and save lives, when the other will not. Now we must consider how far the extra weight of tanks, etc., renders the boat more liable to ship water, and how far it prevents quick evolutions by means of the oars.

It is quite clear to my mind that the lighter a boat is, the better she can avail herself of the right moment to shove off and be propelled to meet a coming roller at the right time, and this is one of the most important elements of success in launching a surf-boat and getting beyond the breakers; after this is accomplished in a strong head wind, more weight would be very valuable—hence a water reservoir to be filled at will would be an excellent adjunct in an iron boat, provided it did not add too much to the weight and cost; when full it would tend to prevent capsizing, it would enable her to keep up the momentum, and it would help materially to right her in the event of being capsized.

Still, the well-founded prejudices of our surf-men against weight should not be ignored, and it should not be forgotten that the chances of keeping a light boat upright may more than overbalance the value of the water bottom. Then comes the question of bringing to the shore a number of extra men—the lighter the boat and the greater the space in her, the more persons she can land; the most dangerous time is in the landing when overloaded, but if the beach be well manned, as is likely, and the crew of the boat be provided with cork belts for themselves and for all she can carry, the chances for ultimate safety are, to my mind, quite as good in the wood shell as in the heavier boat fitted with floats. The question of durability under the effect of exposure to heat and cold must not be lost sight of,—in this the iron boat would have a great advantage; therefore, taking all things into consideration, I recommend the trial of the iron Jersey model boat, with movable floats, delivery valves and end tanks.

Next comes the cedar surf-boat, the vehicle par-excellence, best adapted to insure the confidence of the surf-men, but let her be provided with a cork life-belt for every man of the crew, and one for every extra person she can carry without materially interfering with the management of the boat.

Third, a Beaupré boat should be tested alongside the others.

Fourth, a monitor raft, the valuable qualities of this raft I have tested at Nantucket, in a surf, and I am well convinced that it can be got off and on in a surf when no other boat could live; it cannot be capsized, it cannot be filled unless ruptured, and it can be made to carry out and to land a much greater number of persons than any ordinary surf-boat. At Nantucket I placed on one of two cylinders an anchor weighing 1,200 lbs., besides the wooden stock, and carried it out and landed it with ease; no life-boat, at the time, could have taken out a kedge of 400 lbs. I do not think that in your report you have given sufficient prominence to the monitor raft.

Lastly, it would be well enough in a competitive trial, in rough water, to attempt to launch Lieut. Stodder's boat. If she can be got off the beach and through the breakers in a rough time, she would no doubt do well when beyond them.

As to the Meriam dress, which I see you recommend very highly for all the stations and all the men, not having had any experience of it, I cannot speak confidently as to its utility for general purposes, but I would venture a few remarks on the value of all material of India-rubber, which I have found, after long trial, to be unreliable ; in warm weather it would not be popular with men who require the full use of all their muscles. The cork life-belt, under these conditions, and a cedar boat, would be preferred by surf-men. In cold weather it would be stiff and cumbersome perhaps, and I should, myself, prefer to trust to warm clothing and a cork belt. For service on the beach in launching and awaiting the landing of the boat, it will be found valuable. It will be expensive in first cost, difficult to maintain in good order, and in cold weather it will be uncomfortable. The best test of the value of the Meriam dress will be as to whether the beach-men prefer it *afloat* to a cork life-belt.

I take note of your suggestion to make life-boats of double diagonal planking, like the English and French life-boats. This would doubtless be an improvement, but it would require too much time and money to reduce it to a system. What we want is a light, good modelled and cheap boat, such as can be readily made and repaired by ordinary boat-builders ; as we can have more of these for our money, and transport them with more facility, the end of saving life will be best attained thereby.

In regard to the "life car," originally devised by Captain Ottinger, of the U. S. Revenue Service, but altered and made of iron, under the name of the Francis car, I would say these are too heavy and cumbersome to haul off and on through a surf. There have been instances where it has saved many lives and attained a good name, but I prefer the mode adopted in Europe, which consists of a cork buoy slung to the hawser by a bridle and traveller, and fitted with canvas legs to support a person in a sitting posture. This contrivance is cheap, portable and convenient.

The Coston night signals will be found very useful for illuminating the beach when operating the mortar or rockets and preparing to land shipwrecked persons.

Mr. Samuel Webber has submitted to my inspection a model 30 inches long of an improved Beaupré boat made of tin. The boat to be made after this model of iron is to be 20 feet long, 6 feet 2 inches beam from gunwale to gunwale, depth exclusive of keel 26 inches, sheer 26. She is to have outside air-cases about 5 by 16 inches, and inside air-cases under the thwarts. A platform or deck, constituting a large double bottom or tank, the whole length between the end tanks, which rise to a considerable height above the gunwale, so that the boat is nearly 4½ feet high at the ends; the stem and stern posts are upright, the lines full. The platform is to be perforated by four large automatic delivery valves 6 by 8 inches. She is to have four thwarts to pull eight short oars double bank, and to steer with a sweep. The model is said to be stiff, and to free itself of water readily and to be self-righting, which property in the full-sized boat is to be insured by weight at the keel, which is quite straight. Whether the theory illustrated by the model is to be fully carried out on a large scale remains to be seen.

I visited South Boston to inspect an iron boat made by Mr. Webber, similar, though not identical, with the one described above. She is 20 feet long and weighs about 900 lbs, has large end tanks, a double bottom or deck, constituting an air-case about 8 inches above the bottom in the centre, and 10 inches near the end cases. Also air-cases on the outside, but none under the thwarts at the side, like the model. This boat has four thwarts, and is now fitted to pull four double bank oars and has room for six. The thwarts are not far enough apart to pull freely in rough water, and she is not fitted to steer with a sweep, but may be. I found this boat stiff enough and buoyant enough with six men in her. She pulls fairly, but with this weight in her an inch of water was admitted through the four automatic valves, showing that the air-case in her bottom is not of sufficient capacity to keep her dry with open valves.

She was taken alongside of a small schooner and turned over by a parbuckle, when she righted with considerable water in her, heeling over, so that the water remained in her until a man got into her and brought her upright, when the water *gradually subsided.*

This experiment proved that if capsized with four or five men in her, she would have been very likely to roll over like a log. Mr. Webber attributed the want of self-righting and self-freeing of water to too much dead rise and the absence of weight at the keel to assist in righting her. Without intending to condemn the future full-sized boat to be made like the model, I must say that the one I have seen is a failure, and cannot be considered a life-boat. The boat would be safer and better in all respects if one-third the space under the floor were filled with cork in several compartments, one-third by several air-cases not built into the boat but removable, and about one-third for a water ballast tank, to be filled on getting afloat. This would enable her to dispense with permanent ballast in the shape of an iron keel, and would make her self-righting, and ought to enable her to free herself of water if the valves are large enough and work freely. The construction of the boat tried is very slight, and the double bottom will be very easily punctured, when she would float too deep to pull well in a sea-way. Should Beaupré construct a boat to pull six oars double bank, and make her strong enough to stand the hard work of a life-boat, with cork, air, and water under her floor as suggested, all in separate compartments, and also have the end tanks separate and removable, she would be too heavy and too costly to become popular as a surf-boat, but she would be very good for a passenger steamer.

In connection with safety to steamers burning bituminous coal, and ships carrying the same, to distant markets it may be well to remind ship-owners that means should be provided to detect the heating of such coal and thus to guard against spontaneous combustion. Steamers carrying large masses of soft coal, should have stout iron pipes leading to the bottom of the ship; by letting down a thermometer occasionally, the temperature may be ascertained and measures taken to guard against fire. In short trips across the Atlantic, perhaps there is no appreciable danger of spontaneous combustion, but in longer voyages to the tropics the precaution alluded to will not be found valueless. In sailing vessels carrying large masses of coal, not well ventilated and subject to being wet in the bottom of the ship, there is always great danger of spontaneous combustion. It is a question well worth considering whether such vessels should not be provided with means for ascertaining the heating of the cargo as well as means for quickly arresting the fire when it begins. It seems to me to be quite practicable to guard against fire under these circumstances and at a small expense compared to the extra insurance one has to pay on ships loaded with bituminous coal.

I understand that there are to be erected, and ready for occupation, ten Government Stations by the 1st of December. They are to be located at the following places: Race Point, Provincetown; Peaked Hill Bars, about half-way between Race Point and Highland Light; Highlands, about one mile north of Highland Light;

Parmet Hollow; Cahoon's Hollow, Wellfleet; Nausett; Orleans; Chatham, 1′ south of Lights; Monomoy; and one on the southwest point of Block Island. According to a plan and specifications for the New Jersey and Long Island Stations, furnished me some time ago, I conclude the dimensions of the above named houses, are to be, 42 by 18 feet, with a lower story 9½ feet, and an attic; the ground plan will have a boat-room 29 feet long, and a "living-room," with fire-place, and closets. I understand that when these Stations are fully furnished they will have a boat, mortar and apparatus, bunks for shipwrecked men, and that keepers will be appointed, whose duty will be to take care of the apparatus, and organize crews who shall be on hand in stormy weather ready for any emergency, and that the whole will be under the superintendence of an active agent, who will receive a salary similar to that of the Superintendents on the New Jersey and Long Island shores; but, as the appropriation procured by the Honorable Mr. Buffington is insufficient to fully supply and organize these stations, I conclude that Congress will be called on to give further means for this purpose, before the stations can be completed. I am not aware whether it has been determined to supply these stations with a modified Stodder boat; an iron boat, on the Jersey model with some extra buoyancy; or the ordinary Cedar Boat, so well known on the Jersey shore.

As these stations may be considered in some sense as experimental, as to their general utility, also, as to their boats, and mortars, and their organization; it will be well to have boats of various models, and with various fittings; so that the trained men, who, I understand are to have constant charge, and regular pay, may come to some definite conclusion as to what will be a good boat for each locality.

Extract from a Letter to an Underwriter, dated January 28, 1861.

You know very well that ships and men cannot, in all their essential points of competency, be classed by any existing rule, and a premium charged in accordance therewith. If you were to undertake this task, others would get the premium while you were debating the merits of the risk. A classification of the *block* is necessary, yet that does not always, if generally, regulate the premium; the classification of the *block-head* who is to command is not sufficiently taken into account! You may ask, and generally do ask the owner, "who is going master?" If the reply does not bring to mind a recent loss, a recent trial for cruelty or neglect, or a providential escape from great danger, (incurred by reason of gross carelessness,) and for which the captain has been perhaps rewarded, you accept him as all right; and if the applicant is a good customer, you insure his first-rate ships and his ordinary ships, his first-rate and his ordinary captains, at the same rate of premium for the same voyage, trusting to the laws of chance to make a good average profit.

Marine risks in former times were remunerative, but now there seems to be a general distrust of them, and I think this has arisen mainly for want of a proper scrutiny on the part of insurers upon the main points of the risk, which to my apprehension, are:—

1st. The standing and capacity of the master, particularly in regard to his personal character, and his education as a navigator and his experience in the particular trade he is going into.

2d. The findings and fittings of the ship, particularly in regard to pumps, windlass, capstan, compasses, chronometers, and other instruments, charts, lights, signals, etc., etc.

3d. The number and quality of officers, men, and boys, comprising the crew.

I think it of very little consequence, comparatively, whether the ship class A 1 or B 2, provided the *securities* named above are carefully looked after. I had much rather insure a poor ship with only one chronometer, with a first-rate captain and crew, than an A 1 ship loaded with chronometers, with an incompetent master and crew.

You have inspectors of ships, who take a cursory glance at some of them while building or repairing, and whose opinions are very often made up from the statements of owners or builders, as to their fastenings and general qualifications. You pay these competent and honest agents liberally for making up printed reports, which are very useful as references when you desire to ascertain the facts as to name, rig, port of register, when and where built or repaired, coppered, etc. I believe there are no columns for the name or standing of the captain or owners, which are subjects of momentous interest in estimating the value of marine risks. Besides these, I think you want a place for recording the length and quality of chain cables, for the weight and quality and kind of anchors, and a record as to whether these have been tested, and by what standard.

The comparatively modern custom of building ships and fitting them by contract, "*ready for sea*," has been a fruitful source of disaster, it being the direct interest of the contractor to furnish the cheapest articles of essential utility and safety. Of course there are exceptions to this rule, and these exceptions are among *the ruined contractors.*

Nothing is more common than to see a first-rate ship furnished with anchors which would break if dropped thirty feet upon a rock, and with chains which have never been subjected to the slightest test, and which come from notoriously cheap manufactories in England. Nothing more common than to see iron used for the vital parts of a ship's rigging of the same poor quality as that put into her hull. Nothing more common than to see a fine ship calked by contract, in the very worst weather, and the garboard seam in particular, *when the weight of the ship rests mostly upon the keel blocks*, the result of which is, generally, a leaky ship. Nothing more common than for valuable ships and steamers to be sent to sea without any test of the correctness of their compasses, which, however good in themselves, are liable to be far out by reason of local attraction, and very often with very little attention to the quality of the instruments themselves. Nothing more common than for ships to go to sea without local coast charts, and for masters to be wholly ignorant of harbor navigation, and wholly dependent on pilots, whereby it often happens that much greater risks are incurred, than would be if the captain had a little local knowledge as to his port of destination.

The great improvements, within the last twenty years, in ship's pumps, windlasses, capstans, rig, steering-gear, and in most of the details which make ships safer, when placed by the side of the scale of premiums, and compared with former rates, shows quite clearly that the enhanced value of risks is caused principally by a falling off in the *quality of masters, mates and men, by bad anchors and chains, by bad calking, bad iron work, defective compasses, poor chronometers, a want of good charts, inattention to or ignorance of lunar observations, and a false economy on the part of owners.*

Here is a plan for hoisting and lowering ships' boats, through which they can be managed without the use of yard and stay tackles. It consists simply of two "stanchions" bolted to the side of the ship, attached to which, at the point where they intersect the hammock rail or the hurricane deck, are flat iron davits. Fig. 2, shows the boat in three positions:—A′, ready to lower; B′, stowed for ordinary sea use, or when using the guns; C′, ready to lower on deck, or suspended inboard to avoid the risks of collision. In position A′, the davit may be variously supported; the simplest way perhaps, is as shown by a chain, D′, or by passing the chain through an eye in the head of the davit. At F′, this chain and tackle is shown to hold what is got in moving to the upright position, B′, and also to ease the boat down gradually to position C′.

Fig. 1, shows a fore-and-aft view of the boat stowed in position B′. The davits are kept steady by a permanent spar to which the boat is attached; this spar turns in iron gudgeons working in the ends of the bar davits; it is further steadied in a fore-and-aft direction by permanent guys, D, of rope or chain, which, being set up in a line with the bolt holding the davit to the stanchion, are always "taut." E, represents the gripes, and G, the line of rail; the weight of the boat is partly taken off of the spar and davits by landing in crotches, F, which turn down flat when the boat is to be lowered. The seaman will readily perceive that by this simple arrangement the boats—where the shrouds do not interfere—are always ready to put out or to be taken in. The plan is specially useful for vessels having no yards to hoist the launch or for those with "hurricane" decks. In vessels of the latter class there should be no "fly-rail" abreast of the boats, and they need not come above the plankshire or covering board more than a foot, and may be landed either in permanent or movable chocks.

In vessels-of-war, as is well known, the boats are generally much in the way of damage by the concussion of heavy guns; in saluting they are generally lowered, but in fighting at sea they must be kept in place, not only much exposed to damage by the concussion of one's own guns, but by shot from the enemy; the latter cannot be avoided, and in case of being run into, the boats, as usually stowed, are the first to suffer by the shock. In my plan they can be swung in at a minute's notice, and in case of any disaster, involving the sinking of the ship, the lives of the crew are more likely to be saved by having the heavy boats practically always ready to put into the water; though to speak the simple truth such boats as are universally supplied to war ships are not very good vehicles for saving life, for there is not a *bona fide* "life-boat" in the navy that I know of.

Fig. 1

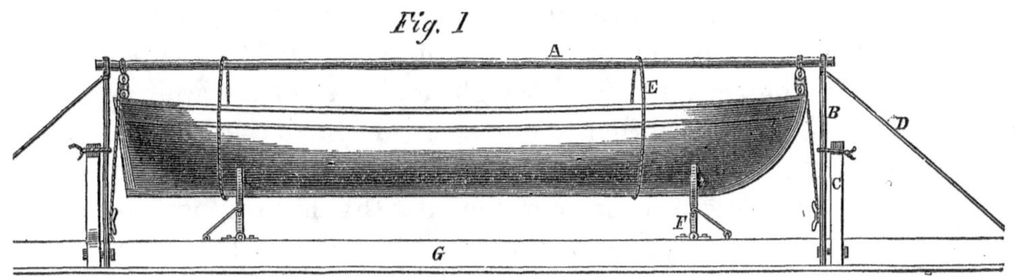

Fig. 2

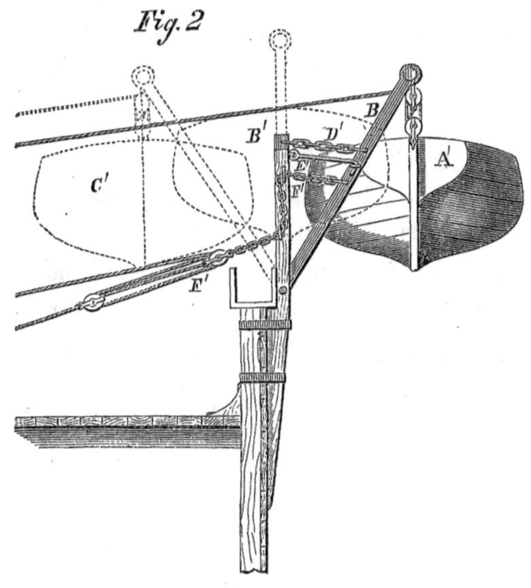

Ship's Boats.

It has often been said that there is not in the whole navy a single life-boat—that is to say, a boat which can never be sunken, and which can be righted when turned over. These are the most essential qualities of a life-boat; more, we cannot well have in ship's boats, on account of the weight and the room required to make them perfect life-boats. We shall be told by naval men that it is very easy, at short notice, to convert any boat into a life-boat by lashing water-breakers somewhere in the interior. This will answer to prevent sinking too deep to be bailed out; but, if lashed low down, they would assist her turning bottom up, and keep her so, in a surf or sea-way. We therefore repeat, there are no life-boats in the navy. As we cannot carry perfect life-boats at the davits, we must devise the most simple means for making boats somewhat insubmergible and easy to right when turned over.

Boats for war vessels must have room for arms, ammunition and supplies. In what we propose to say, we desire our readers to understand that we go for *working boats*, and not mere pleasure boats. We think every boat can afford space for an air-tank at each end, varying in size according to size of the boat. This will be very useful in assisting to righten the boat, and if it has a man-hole, it can be used as a safe place of deposit for valuable traps, as signal lights or papers, not occupying sufficient space to impair its utility as a float. And under the thwarts, at the side, in double bank boats, and amidships in single bank, there should be some floating power, as cork or air cannisters, sufficient in buoyancy with the help of the end cannisters to keep the boat in condition to be bailed out if filled by shipping water, or partly full when righted. This is all we can expect to attain in a ship's boat.

All ship's boats, whether for merchant service or for the navy, should have a centre-board, and no projection of keel. In suggesting this to a naval friend, he answers: "For one or two boats, officers would appreciate the centre-board; launches are generally propelled by steam, and are supposed to be capable of towing all the other boats, so as to spare the men." And he also says: "Boats of men-o'-war are fitted with lug-sails, and these are regarded as only to be used when the boat will lay her course; beating to windward is usually not allowed, partly on account of the insufficiency of the rig, and partly because pulling is a good physical exercise; a lug does not lumber a boat, and does very well with a free wind; for beaching, the absence of keel will be a great advantage."

Presuming this to be the general reasoning of naval men, we would say that a properly cut and properly set lug-sail is as good as any ship's boat can have, and with the aid of centre-board, will be *weatherly, sure in stays, safe to go on a beach, easy to stow* within another boat and at the davits, will turn more quickly under sail or oars; in short, she will be more safe and more manageable in all respects than a keel boat. If beating dead to windward is out of order, the rule is the result of poor fittings. It cannot be out of order to make good the courses, instead of making several points lee-way. If it is recognized as good economy to husband the strength of the men for great efforts by towing under steam, there can be no objection to exercising the same economy by doing *well* what we now do *very badly* for want of centre-boards and properly fitted lug-sails.

In a cutter 30 feet long, there is room for masts of 18 feet, without interfering with the stern-sheets. The fore and main-sails may be exactly alike; the latter has a light boom, which is necessary to make it set well. The fore-yard is two feet longer than the main, in order to set on it a jib, representing a split-lug. This is a valuable auxiliary in tacking as well as in balancing the canvas. The jib is not necessarily a fixture, but may often be dispensed with; still, when reefed with the others, it will be found very effective in stays.

In what is called a whaleboat in a frigate, though not like one except in general shape, the sprits come to the tack of the sail and shove into a pocket 5 or 6 feet up, so that, when brailed to the mast, you have practically a reefed sail of the shape called "shoulder of mutton." The principal advantage attained by bringing the tack of a lug-sail to the mast is that it needs no dipping.

In the Journal for October, 1855, I find a valuable paper on the management of boats in a surf, from which I extract some hints, which, like those for rescuing drowning men, require practice rather than theory. At the same time, no harm can arise by making use of the experience of the writer. In discussing this subject, I would remark that beaches differ almost as much as roads; some are steep-to, with little current, others with cross-currents, others running off shoal and regular, others intersected by bars and gullies; so that, in laying down rules for manœuvring in a surf, it has to be borne in mind that the boat must be adapted to the locality, and the men themselves must be acquainted with it. No general rule will answer for every place, and we cannot have a boat adapted to all. Men accustomed to whaleboats, pulling long oars, are not the best for double bank oars, and those who have been accustomed to dories, pulling short oars cross handed, if put into a whale-boat, would be out of place. With this preface, I shall quote so much from the Journal as will illustrate the subject:

In conversing with our beach men, I find that they prefer a light, fast-pulling, flat midship-section boat, for the following reasons: time being precious, they can transport them to the scene of action readily with few men; they can shove them off and get headway on them to pass a coming roller before it breaks, or they can back astern to avoid a "coamer" much quicker than in a heavy boat. If the boat is slightly rounding on the flat bottom, or what is called rocker bottom, she can be slewed to meet or to avoid a coming sea *by the steersman*, without *the necessity*, as in a large boat, of being simultaneously assisted by the oars. The latter is a delicate operation, seldom well done except by a thoroughly drilled crew. In fact, the safety of a boat in going off-shore depends almost altogether on the management of the steer oar. In coming in before the sea it is still the most important thing, but in this case the oarsmen, when facing the sea, can more readily assist the steersman. The fact that the fewer the men operating a boat in a dangerous sea the more chance for safety, is well illustrated in the dory, which, for the information of "outside barbarians," I will describe. They are very light, flat, rocker bottomed skiffs with considerable sheer, and sides flaring out to the gunwale; the bow is sharp, and the stern cut off so as to leave the end about 18 inches or 2 feet across; the flat of the bottom is perhaps half the beam from gunwale to gunwale; they differ in size, so that fishermen carry them in nests three together, some pulling four short oars by two men and some only two. Now, as the smallest of these shells when once off the beach are controlled by one mind, one impulse, and controlled very quickly, it follows that they can get off and on, meeting heavy rollers before they break, or backing astern to avoid breakers, when very few surf-boats could go ; but they are so crank and easily overloaded, that they are quite useless in boarding wrecks to bring inexperienced persons to the shore. In a larger dory, pulling four oars, the chance of mismanagement is increased, although the power to pull to windward is doubled. In proportion, therefore, as we increase the size and the number of men, we increase the chances of mistakes. Still, the necessity exists to have boats capable of bringing to the shore several persons besides the crew. We must therefore have experienced men for crews ; if possible, men who have been accustomed to operate together, men who can understand what the steersman requires of them and act simultaneously. If a boat is to be manned in a harbor, and intended to be pulled to sea over a bar where there is sufficient broken water at all times, there is no objection to a large double-bank boat to pull ten or twelve oars ; but to go off a shelving beach in a rough time, such a boat will never be popular with our surf-men.

Management of Boats in a Surf and Broken Water.

The management of a boat in the dangerous circumstances of a heavy sea and broken water is so practical a thing, that it may be thought no rules or instructions can be given which would be of much value to those called on to put them in execution. Experience alone can give that confidence and presence of mind and skill which are indispensable to safety.

Nevertheless, as all our boatmen are not equally skilful, and as the majority of other sailors have no experience in the managing of boats in a surf, we propose to offer some recommendations, not the result of our own experience alone, but of that collected from various parts of our coasts.

In offering our opinion in so important a matter, on which life or death will often depend, we desire to do so with all deference to those who have already experience for a guide, who, having a practical knowledge of the particular character of the sea and surf in their own localities, and of their own boats, have learned that particular management which has appeared most suitable to them. They will be able to compare our suggestions with their experience, and will then be guided by their own judgment in a matter wherein their own safety is concerned; but they are not the persons for whose use our recommendations are more especially offered.

When it is considered how various is the character of broken water, according as it is on a beach, in a tide-way, in the bar of a river, or the edge of a shoal, how it will vary according to the steepness or flatness of the shore, the relative directions of the current or the wind, and of the wind and the shore. And when the variety in the build and size of boats in different localities is remembered, the conclusion will be come to, that no one rule will be applicable to meet all cases; that the same rule will not apply alike to all boats; that it will not apply alike to the irregular sea on the edge of a shoal, to the long and steady rollers advancing in parallel lines on the open beach on exposed parts of the coast, or to the short and dangerous sea occasioned by the set of tides. There will be special peculiarities to be consulted at every locality which will call for some deviation in detail from any general rule, yet on the other hand, there are undoubtedly some leading principles which are more or less applicable to all, and which should therefore be ever borne in mind.

With a view to ascertain the results of local experience, and as to how far any general rule might apply, the Committee of the National Life-boat Institution caused a series of questions on the "management of boats in a surf and broken water" to be printed and circulated. To these, replies were received from 128 different places on the coasts of the United Kingdom; and they contain a large amount of valuable information.

In our observations on the subject, we propose to state the substance of the information thus obtained on the different points of management, and to add our own comments upon them.

We will premise that our remarks chiefly refer to open boats, which are managed either by oars alone, or indifferently with sails and oars.

Our subject will then be arranged into two divisions, viz., the proper management on going off from the shore against a heavy sea, and that on running before a surf or heavy broken sea for the land.

Whilst on some questions a curious contrast of opinion on the same points may be observed even at places contiguous to each other, yet on one point, viz , as to the relative amount of danger on going off against a head sea, and on running before it, the opinion is almost unanimous; that the greater danger exists when running before, or away from a sea; also, that this greater danger arises from the liability of boats to broach-to; if the sea be heavy they are upset. Another point on which nearly all agree is, that open boats under sail, before entering the broken water, on running for the land, should take in their sails and go through under oars.

The question on management was as follows: in rowing to windward, would you give a boat all possible speed against a heavy broken sea on its approach; and when running before one, would you do the same away from it, or would you check the boat's way until it had passed?

The replies were thus divided:

On going off, 18 were in favor of giving all speed; 81 in favor of checking speed.

On running before a sea, 27 in favor of giving all speed; 71 in favor of checking speed.

It will be observed that the opinions are on these points more conflicting than might have been anticipated; as, however, there can be but one right way to manage boats placed in similar circumstances, it follows that either the boatmen at some parts of the coasts are unacquainted with the proper management, or that there are local circumstances which make it vary at different places; probably both of these causes must be referred to in order to account for the disparity above displayed.

On the first point, that of going off through broken water, the replies are of four kinds: 1. Give all speed possible. 2. Check speed. 3. Keep steerage-way on the boat. 4. Avoid the sea by watching for a smooth.

On the second point, of running for the shore, the replies are: 1. Check speed as much as possible. 2. Give all speed possible. 3. Bring all weights aft, and keep the boat well down by the stern. 4. Tow astern a pig of ballast or other weight, or a hollow conical canvas bag called a "drogue." 5. Watch opportunity and avoid the sea. 6. Keep steerage-way on the boat. 7. If under sail, run in under small head-sail only. 8. In sail, and take the boat in under oars. 9. Steer with an oar. 10. Turn the bow round to the sea and back in stern foremost.

On the first point, the majority of places where the seamen are noted for skill and experience are in favor of giving a boat all the speed possible on going off. On the second point, it is their custom to check a boat's way when running, and to row back against each heavy sea until it has passed, then to follow it in, repeating the operation.

A singular exception to the above rule is Deal, where the boatmen are notoriously courageous and experienced, and where their custom appears to be exactly the reverse of the above, giving all speed on running before a sea, and checking speed on going off against it. It appears, however, that several boats have been lost at Deal by broaching-to and upsetting when running before a sea. On the first point, going off against a sea, the custom may be resolved into two kinds—to give all speed through a broken sea, and to check speed on the immediate approach of a heavy wave. Again, the rule to avoid a sea is only applicable to places where, from the steepness of the shore, the sea does not break until close to it, when boats, by the right opportunity being watched for, may often avoid the worst of the sea; where, however, the shore is flat, and the sea breaks at a quarter of a mile or more from the beach, a boat must of necessity encounter a succession of seas before she is clear of the broken water on going off, and after she has entered it on running for the land.

The danger on going off is of two kinds, 1st, the risk of being overwhelmed by the sea breaking over the boat and filling her. 2ndly, of being driven back by the sea and turned end over end, or turned round broadside to the sea and capsized by the same or the following wave before she can be got head to the sea again. The first danger will be more or less imminent in proportion to the size of the boat and the height of her bow as compared with the magnitude of the waves. If the boat be small, with a low bow, it would be folly to row her right into the crest of a heavy roller at the moment of its curling over, as it would then fall into and fill the boat. The preferable management would doubtless be, if possible, so to place her as that each sea should break a little ahead of her. The second danger will be the more imminent the less way there is on the boat, and the fuller and bluffer her bow; it would probably also be greater in a light than a heavy boat, the cause being that the boat not having sufficient speed or *inertia* to carry her up the ascent of the approaching wave, and over its crest, she is carried back by it, and may then, if a short boat, be turned instantly end over end, if a long one, be driven down stern foremost, or turned broadside to the sea, and capsized by the same or the next wave. On this point our opinion as to the management is, that in a small boat, if possible, the seas should be avoided until after breaking, but if they cannot be so, that the utmost speed which oars can effect should be given to the boat; whilst in larger boats, and in life-boats, which are not in the same danger of swamping, the utmost speed should invariably be given; indeed, we feel persuaded that the safety of a boat will often depend, in a really heavy sea, on preserving her headway, and that the wide or bluff boat, which cannot retain its headway, is, for that reason, often more unsafe than a narrower and sharper boat.

On the second point, running before a broken sea, an equal variety of management is observable, yet all intended to meet the one great risk of "broaching-to," which nearly all agree in considering to be the greatest danger to which a boat can be exposed, and to be that which calls for the most skill and management to obviate it.

The greater number of boatmen on the coast are in the habit of checking a boat's way through the water, or of backing her against a heavy sea. Their practice is to stop the boat's way by backing their oars until the crest of the wave has struck the boat's stern and passed her midship part, then to give way again, running in on the back of that wave, as far as they may be able to, and repeating the same operation until they arrive at the beach, being careful, by steering with oars at the quarter or stern, to keep the boat, as far as possible, end on to the direction in which the sea is running. In a sailing boat this principle can only be so far acted on as to diminish the boat's speed through the water by taking her in under a very reduced amount of sail, which is commonly done, and by towing weights or instruments made for the purpose.

The steering with an oar on each quarter is another expedient, employed to prevent broaching-to, as, when running, a boat will not answer her helm on being overtaken by a sea.

The recommendation to watch for an opportunity and avoid a sea, equally in running as on going off, could only be practiced at those localities where the beach is steep.

In reply to the question as to whether any particular kinds of boats are more liable than others to broach-to, the answers given are so conflicting as to afford no information on the point.

Broaching-to may be correctly accounted for as follows: "On a boat encountering a heavy broken sea or roller end on, if she be stationary or is being propelled in a contrary direction to the wave, she will receive its blow, and it will quickly pass by her, her own inertia preventing her being carried away by it. If, however, she is being propelled in the same direction as the waves, and running rapidly through the water with her stern towards them, on a wave overtaking her, its first effect is to throw her stern up and to depress her bow, when she offers so slight resistance to it that she is hurried along with it, her stern high up immersed in the crest of the sea, and her bow down at its base; as the wave approaches shoaler water, its inshore surface approaches more and more nearly to a perpendicular, and the tendency of the boat to run down this steep inclination, added to the momentum she has already from her previous motion, causes her to run her bow under water, when her buoyancy at that end being destroyed, her stern is pressed onward by the summit of the wave, and she is instantly, if a short boat, turned "end over end," or if a long one, capsized quarter-wise. If she have so high a bow that it does not become altogether immersed, or if, as in a life-boat, the end of the boat is occupied by a water-tight air-case to the height of the gunwale, so as to prevent the admission of the water over the bow, the effect then is that the boat is instantaneously turned round broadside to the sea, when again, unless she be a life-boat of a superior description, she is almost certain to be upset. In the circumstances thus described, the sole cause of a boat's running herself under water or broaching-to, is that of running from a sea instead of awaiting it, and suffering it to pass by. If, on the other hand, the wave passes the boat, as its crest advances from the stern to the fore part, the stern is thrown out of the water; steering oars are therefore a most valuable auxiliary aid when running before a sea.

After the danger of broaching-to has passed, there remains the lesser danger of beaching. The general custom appears to be, that where the beach is more or less steep, she is steered into it in an oblique direction, the bow being turned partially round towards that direction from which the sea is running. If, however, the shore be very flat, she is steered perpendicularly to the beach.

We have now only to offer our own opinion and recommendations on the subject for the use of those who have not already experience and skill for their guides, and for the consideration of those who have. Amongst the former we would especially address ourselves to the crews of merchant vessels, who, having to desert their ships from any cause, may attempt to land on the open coast.

1st. On going off from the shore against a heavy broken sea, whether from the beach on an open coast, or over the bar of a river, and whether the beach be steep or flat, no boat which is not of sufficient size and power, in proportion to the nature of the sea, to offer some chance of safety, will be taken off. In any such boat, unless from the steepness of the beach and nature of the sea, she can, by skilful management, be made to avoid it by watching a favorable opportunity, the safest plan is to give her all the speed which can be obtained by rowing.

2nd. On the management of a boat, when running through broken water for the land, our opinion is that the greatest danger consists in following the natural impulse to escape from the seas as rapidly as possible; no boat can be propelled so fast but that the waves will overtake her. Our recommendations then are, 1st, Before entering broken water, if a sail be set take it in, unship the mast, and lash both, with any other spare gear, to the thwarts of the boat, to prevent it falling over on the lee side, if the boat should be struck by a sea and thrown on her beam ends. Next, if the boat be a square-sterned one, turn her round with her head to the sea; then row or back her in, carefully keeping her, both with the aid of the rudder and oars, end on to the sea. Watch each sea as it advances, and check the boat's progress, by rowing or backing the oars, until the brow of the wave has passed the centre of the boat, then go in on the back of it, if it can be done, but keeping a constant lookout behind for the coming up of the next wave, when the same operation has to be repeated. Even with these precautions the sea may be so overwhelming, or the boat so inferior, that they may fail to save her, but we conceive them to be her only means.

As regards the crews of merchant vessels leaving their ships and attempting to land in their own boats, we recommend that they should not take to a boat as long as there might be any chance of safety in their ship, especially in the night time; that if not fitted up as a life-boat, they should secure, if there should be time to do so, some small empty casks, tightly corked, under the thwarts, and in the head and stern-sheets of the boat; that if the vessel should be provided with any life-buoys or life-belts, the former should be taken in the boat, and the latter be worn by themselves. That on leaving their vessel they should, if practicable, make for the nearest harbor or other sheltered place in preference to attempting a landing on the open coast; even if the weather should be fine, or the wind off the land, as there often is a surf on the beach in such situations that would be dangerous to ordinary ships' boats, even in calm and fine weather.

We cannot conclude this humble effort to render a service to the boatmen and other seamen who may be exposed to risk on our own coasts or elsewhere, without addressing a few words to shipowners in case it should come to their notice.

We think that they would be rendering an important service by endeavoring to afford their servants every reasonable protection to their lives in case of shipwreck, or the necessity for taking to their boats. It would not put any owner to a very great expense to fit up one boat in his vessel as a life-boat, or, so far a life-boat that she should not founder with her crew in if filled by a sea. It would not put him to a very great expense to furnish a life-buoy to his vessel, and as many good life-belts as the number of his crew. These trifling things supplied to all vessels, as they ought to be, would be the means of saving many a poor fellow's life; the supplying them would not only be a duty to humanity, but an act of policy.

I also notice in the same Journal, a suggestion of Lieut. E. G. Butler, R. N., in regard to means to be attached to the bottom of boats, by which when capsized the crew can hold on and thus assist to right them. He suggests placing a rod along the bottom near the keel to which life-lines are attached; he thinks, these would not interfere materially with the speed of the boat.

I suggest that metallic rods near the keel, will get out of order and be difficult to reach unless the life-lines are so long as to be an incumbrance; I would therefore recommend, that the bilge-battens, generally placed say two feet from the keel, be made a little thicker, and be provided with short life-lines which can be more readily grasped by men in the water and will be nearly as efficient in righting the boat as the others.

Some valuable hints to men going to the rescue of drowning or drowned persons, may be gathered from a paper in the *British Nautical Magazine* for Sept. 1870, originally published in the *Life Boat Journal*. While this operation can only be done well, by those who have practiced the rules, these hints may be of some value to those who go overboard without previous experience, to save their fellow men: these form the rule while the exceptions are among men who are perfectly at home in the water. The writer says:—

RESCUE OF LIFE BY SWIMMING, AND EXPERIMENTS THEREON.

The accompanying paper is from remarks, by M. Ferrand, member of the Lyons Board of Health. He was deputed by the French Government to re-organize the system of life-buoys in that country, the insufficiency of which had too often been made palpable. "While looking at the great display of the resources of civilized nations, my subject leads me to speak of a feat which, to my mind, has a peculiar magnificence,—I mean rescue by a man, without life-belt or rope, but stripped for the emergency; the man who, with no aid but his own courage, throws himself into the waves to save the life of a fellow-creature at the risk of his own life. The difficulty of this operation is generally very great, but it appears to me to be increased to an enormous extent, so as to render abortive many attempts, through ignorance of the best method of accomplishing the rescue of a drowning person.

"I have frequently questioned retired boatmen of the Rhone, Saone, and elsewhere, all tried men for courage and skill, and their unanimous reply has been: 'a drowning man must be taken hold of as best possible: you are lucky if you can simply support him, if a boat or a rope is seen at hand; in the absence of these you must either push him on before you, or drag him, according to circumstances.' But, I answered, what happens if you are unable to hold the head of the drowning man long enough out of water? 'Suffocation takes place while he is in your hands.'

"The method which has most interested me is that performed by an Englishman named Hodgson, of Sunderland; and after having experimented on and developed it, I recommend it for its precision and efficacy. It consists in holding the drowning man by the hair, and turning him on his back. Then the salvor turns over rapidly with his face upwards, places the head of the man on his breast, and thus swims to land. This method is so simple and easy, that in an experiment which I had the pleasure of making this autumn with my friend Dr. Bron, I was able with ease to practice simultaneously the rescue of two persons more or less motionless.

"The drowning man, then, should be held with the left hand, his face, and his face only, being out of water. If he is bald, support him by the beard or chin, or even by the top of his coat collar. Keep your right hand free to help you in swimming, or to take more secure hold of ropes or boats, if any be near for if the shore cannot be gained you can support yourself thus in the water for several hours.

"I have thus examined the easiest case, that of the fainting, or at least motionless drowned man, but I will next discuss the case that I have found full of anxiety, that of saving a man who, without help, must certainly die, and who struggles with the energy of despair. All English and other rescuers invariably answer, 'don't touch him; the sacrifice of your life will be useless; wait till he becomes calm; which happens after the first spasm.' This waiting may be prudent up to a certain point, but it appears to me particularly cruel. If two hours of care and effort are sometimes necessary to restore a drowned man to life, it often requires but a minute to make him a dead man. The desperate clutch of the dying man undoubtedly has its dangers, but only if you allow yourself to be seized first. As a man loses consciousness he gradually releases his hold of the object which he has seized with his clenched hand. I object, then, to that excessive prudence which is recommended, as it may be attended with serious consequences.

"Don't let yourself be seized, I said but I must add, be ready to seize the drowning man rapidly from behind him, and at two points simultaneously, to render his body, as far as possible, motionless. Keeping the face out of water, seize him at the same time by the hair with the left hand, and by the right shoulder with the right hand. Thus keep him at a distance, your arms extended in front and your body in an upright position; then take care of his right arm, and if he throws himself about, if he seeks a point of support which may prevent your turning him on his back, seize this arm because that is the part easiest to take firm hold of, and place it forcibly on your left hand behind his head. Very quickly, as will easily be conceived, the two hands of the dying man will fix themselves instinctively on the left hand of the rescuer. If the case is otherwise, if the hands of the man are fastened closely on the side of him who comes to snacth him from death, it does not matter. The rescuer is bound not to return alone. His head is kept free from all surprise, and his legs are out of reach.

"When the drowning man has sunk to the bottom he often reappears once or twice on the surface, and by that time, when he is reached, his exhausted strength renders him by no means dangerous; and in all cases, the muscular relaxation having destroyed all his tightness of grasp, the process of taking him to land has no longer the violent character of which I have just spoken. If the man you are saving is conscious, encourage him, sustain him a minute with your outstretched arm while taking hold of him by one of the armpits; tell him to keep his legs stretched out, as you are going to place his head on your breast, and carry him off in complete safety.

"But the third situation, which causes me most anxiety, is that of the man who dives, and who by reason of the refracting medium in which he finds himself, distinguishes only with difficulty the uncertain shape of the drowning man, who is moving about at the bottom; he may then be surprised and seized at random. The judicious boldness of the rescuer must then make him consider the time that passes away, for the danger exists only during the first moments.

"It is not without reason that I persist in saying that however perilous be the situation, the proceeding which consists in taking hold of a drowning man who is unconscious, or who has not come to his full senses, is perfectly and readily practicable.

"To enforce this point, I invite the reader to follow the narration of the experiences which I subjoin.

" It is well known that a body plunged into the water has its weight diminished by a quantity equal to the weight of the quantity of water displaced by the body; let us see what is the quantity of water displaced by the drowning man. According to my experience, an adult weighing one hundred and fifty pounds displaces about eighteen gallons, and therefore weighs no more than about four pounds when submerged. If the head is out of water, the volume displaced is less, and the weight is augmented by from eight to twelve pounds. This is a weight easily borne, varying with different persons.

" I have said that this quantity was variable, according to the individuals; with young subjects, or those who are lean and withered, the specific gravity is higher. By keeping nothing but the face of the drowning man out of the water, the weight can be reduced to six pounds.

" The trunk of the body has then very nearly the same specific gravity as water; but during life, and especially when long breaths are taken, it becomes lighter than water.

" If the question is raised, as to whether the position of the rescuer lying on his back is quite necessary, I answer that I recommend it after thorough study. In considering their exact advantages, I have come to the following conclusions:—In swimming on the back, I easily practiced the simultaneous rescue of two adults whose heads were placed on my breast; and in another experiment, I found it impracticable to save a single youth of fifteen years old resting on my shoulders, swimming in the ordinary way. To show how far the first named experiment could be carried, I performed the following experiment: a weight of twenty-four to thirty pounds placed on the chest of the swimmer was easily supported above the surface of the water; whilst attached to the nape of the neck or to the shoulders he was soon obliged to place himself in an upright position in order to get breath. In other words, it was simply like fastening a stone to the neck to drown one's self.

" One of these two positions then was defective, that of swimming on the stomach. Why is this? for it seems to be more natural and preferable, especially as offering the aid of the two arms to swimming, and of being able to see in front. I think the explanation is to be found in the estimate of weights which I have just given, proving that he who swims in the most customary manner, on the stomach, is really heavier than he who swims on his back. The difference is in the man himself, for, in the ordinary way, he has to bear the weight of his own head in addition to his burden, whilst in swimming on the back, the head is submerged all but the face, and the weight which the swimmer has to support becomes less. Scientific estimates may be called in to the support of swimming on the back. Is it not a scientific fact, that a body plunged into a liquid undergoes from this liquid a vertical pressure equal to the volume of the liquid which it displaces ? Now, in swimming on the stomach, this pressure compresses the chest, which is the dilatable part, and thus renders most painful the deep inspirations required after prolonged efforts.

" Is it not certain that the stability of a floating body is so much the greater in proportion to the lowness of position of the centre of gravity ?

" In swimming on the back, the rescuer has more stability, his chest is more dilatable, his respiration less difficult, his specific gravity lightened by the greatest possible introduction of exterior air ; he is free from every obstacle, and his hands being so much freer, easily sustain and protect him whose life he wishes to save.

" To discover the point where a drowned man is, who has disappeared in calm water, the bubbles of air which rise to the surface are a sure indication for the diver.

" Finally. Such is my confidence in the method above described that I desire to make it known by all possible means, and above all, by the practice of my directions in all swimming schools. In effect, I propose to make as many men capable of saving their fellow-men as there are swimmers, and thus to augment the chances of safety for all who are in peril of drowning."

Miscellaneous.

The Journal of the "National Life-Boat Association" for January, 1870, contains an able article concerning the mercantile marine of Great Britain. In reading it carefully I cannot but be struck with the fact that we are suffering from the same or similar causes. In quoting therefrom somewhat liberally, it will be realized how similar are the conditions under which Great Britain and the United States legislate for political objects and manufactures, to the neglect of the commerce of the sea. I have condensed the language of the writer as much as possible, without impairing the sense, and beg pardon in advance for the liberty I take.

The "British Public" has manifested a considerable degree of dissatisfaction at the state of the Mercantile Marine; a dissatisfaction none the less real because it can hardly be said to have assumed a tangible form. Or, perhaps, that the writers have dealt with particular evils, instead of holding surveys of the whole subject, and have combined this mode of dealing with such an evident display of animosity towards some particular class, who in their opinion is to blame, as to shake the faith of uninitiated impartial readers in the existence of any evils at all.

Thus we have one class of speakers and writers blaming the House of Commons, whose members, they assert are "grossly ignorant of, and indifferent to the whole matter." Such persons must be reminded, that the House of Commons is the scrutinizer and rejecter of laws, rather than the framer of them; and that all laws relating to particular interests, must emanate from the class or profession itself in the first instance, and only in exceptional cases can the House be expected to help a particular body or interest, without its members having previously expressed that they require the legislature to interfere.

Another class say that the Board of Trade is at fault; that with all possible means of information at their disposal, they may be expected to draw up regulations which would meet every evil. "Why," say they, "does the Board always move so slowly? and why, when it does move, is there always so much left to futurity?" But, it must be remembered that the Board of Trade is what the nation has made it, and what at present, it wills it to remain. It is, in fact, composed of two distinct parts, which must of necessity be frequently as widely as the poles, in thought and opinion on every conceivable point of public duty. These two parts we may divide into the permanent or working staff, and the parliamentary leaders. Now, as the political head changes with the ministry, it cannot be expected that the views of any president will exactly coincide with those of his predecessor or successor; and so we can easily conceive, that the elaborate scheme of reform, prepared under the auspices of a whig leader, and prepared, too, with infinite care and wisdom by the permanent officials, may yet be so opposed to the views of a tory successor, or *vice versa*, that it may never see the light at all, or be so mutilated as to be robbed of half its power and meaning.

Again, one president may, as a Member of Parliament, have for his constituents the men of some great northern seaport, and influenced by their views of some point of sorely-needed reform, he may give certain bias to the laws he is preparing for the approval of Parliament; but while the proposed measure is still not law—lo, the ministry changes! Well, the in-coming president has for his constituents the leading men of the port of London, who are pretty certain to regard the question from a totally different point of view; and so, whatever may be his own views, the new man has to choose between the favor of his electors, or the destruction of the bill. That the officials are anxious to do all in their power to remedy existing evils in the mercantile marine, the elaborate "Merchant Shipping Bill for 1870" sufficiently proves.

There is also a considerable number of persons, who speak and write as though every wreck were to be directly traced to the incompetence or carelessness of masters of merchant ships, and who hold them up to public opprobrium, as monsters of brutality. There are, no doubt, drunken and incompetent persons to be found in command of merchant ships; but we cannot admit there is a greater proportion so placed than may be met with in other walks of life. That there is a considerable number of persons intrusted with command at sea, who are wofully deficient in education, cannot be denied; and possibly no people more deeply deplore the deficiency than the members of the profession themselves; but here, as in many other points connected with this subject, the nation and the nation's rulers are to blame. Many years ago, a special means of education at the national expense should have been provided,—a means of training youthful aspirants, and a means of completing in later years the training of older officers

It may be asked "Why should the officers of the merchant service be treated with more consideration than the members of any other profession, who are not servants of the state?" We reply that the mercantile marine is so intimately associated with the vital interests of the nation that it must always stand alone in its relation to the general public.

Not that we propose that gentlemen intended for the merchant service should be educated solely at the public expense, any more than we should consider it a reasonable proposition, that henceforth students intended for the bar or the church should be received at the universities free of charge; but we do think that somewhat similar institutions should long ago have been called into existence for the benefit of the merchant service. Not only does the rapid development of science, in its application to the requirements of navigation, demand such an institution, but the best interests of the nation would be effectually served by its establishment. Moreover, it is tolerably certain that nothing but that isolation from his fellows, and that want of opportunity to discuss and make known his wants, which has ever been the peculiar misfortune of the sailor, has prevented members of the merchant service from forcing this question on public attention and eliciting those substantial marks of sympathy which the occasion would seem to require.

The country, in fact, never has duly recognized its obligations to the mercantile marine, and has always practically ignored the right it possesses to one of the first places in the nation's regard. In exact accordance with the decay or prosperity of the mercantile marine, and with it, the safety of her merchandise, the stability of her merchants, and the ability of the country to produce at any moment the largest number of good sailors in the world, must ever be the decrease or otherwise of this country's safety, credit, and wealth.

As to the sense that is shown of this great obligation we are under to the officers and men of our merchant navy, let the daily records of vessels sent to sea to be lost; of vessels improperly provisioned; of vessels with insufficient accommodation for their crews; of vessels with barely half the crew they ought to have; of vessels with no medical necessaries; of vessels with neither life-belts or boats, or with bad ones; of vessels sent on long voyages short of water, short of food, and badly commanded: let these things answer that question. Let the true description of any of our great seaports bear witness also; and the fact that the great mass of our sailors have ever been the prey of their fellow-subjects on shore, while until very recently the legislature has seemed to consider this to be the natural order of things, and that they were not responsible for the scandal. Let the fact that crews have been, and until very lately, without hindrance, on their return from long voyages, drugged, and robbed, and reshipped drunk, in open day; the fact that no care is taken by the State to educate the officers, or to keep up the supply of the men, and that year by year the proportion of British-born sailors is decreasing, and the proportion of avoidable wrecks is increasing; let these things show how nobly the nation recognizes its obligations to the merchant service.

But the most hardly used people of all are the shipowners. Who remembers that they, of all people, have the most to gain by an efficient mercantile marine, and in the long run, the most to lose by the continuation of the present state of things? Can it be doubted that the majority of our shipowners would gladly inaugurate reform, if only they saw the way to carry it into effect? Or is it not reasonable to suppose that if they, who must know better than the public exactly what is wrong, and to what extent, do not remedy existing evils, or at least try to do so, it is simply because they are so placed that they cannot? Can it be doubted, for instance, that the shipowners would prefer that their ships should be manned by British seamen, if only they could be found in sufficient numbers, and if they could he placed on a par with foreign seamen (now so extensively employed) in the point of sobriety and steadiness—that they would hail with joy the day when they could be sure their ships were putting to sea well-manned and well-commanded, instead of knowing, as they too often do now, that their vessels are being towed out to sea with crews on board who, partly from their different nationalities, partly from disease and partly from intoxication, are ill-prepared to meet the emergencies induced by storms and difficult navigation.

So long as an owner has power to insure his vessel for her full value, there will always be a considerable number of persons who are entirely unconcerned as to the ultimate fate of their ships; yet we must believe that there are numbers more who look at the question from a wider and higher point of view, and who are as deeply concerned at loss of life or property, which could have been prevented by better crews and better outfits, as the most patriotic citizen.

The fact is, shipowners are beset with many special difficulties, which are not generally taken into consideration; every improvement, whether in the ships or the men, must be a question of profit and loss; and it is an unfortunate truth that it must be one of direct loss to the owner. Whether the reform take the shape of entering and training up lads for sailors, or the placing better found ships at sea, or devoting more space to the accommodation of the crews, or whatever else we may wish to see carried out, it must be paid for out of the pockets of the owners, who introduce the measure first into their ships; and so long as these owners continue this practice, they must be working at a loss, and be content with the pleasure of introducing reforms for the general good at the price of ruin to themselves. Certain owners dwelling in one end of the kingdom hold peculiar views on certain measures, and these views are steadily opposed by owners dwelling at the other end; so that such measures would never be introduced but by a Board of Trade, politically powerful, and independent enough to set one-half of the entire shipping interest at defiance. When have we had such a Board, and who is the strong-handed reformer, able and willing to devise and administer laws, dealing equal justice to owners and underwriters, sailors and officers, together with all possible protection to the public?

"Well, if all this be so, and no one is to blame, things are already at their best! We must make up our minds to the decay in numbers of British-born seamen and the increase in numbers of avoidable wrecks."

We reply,—no; that is not our meaning. On the contrary, every nerve should be strained to bring about wholesale reform; to insure all classes of ships being sent to sea well—thoroughly well-found; to insure their being all commanded by perfectly competent persons; to insure their all being provided with proper, not sham, means of saving life. Every effort should be made to induce a healthier tone in the shipping transactions at the Royal Exchange, and to eliminate, as far as possible, the swindling element from the necessary and ordinary business transacted with marine insurers. Much, also, can be done by legislation to decrease the number of wrecks; much, undoubtedly, will be effected by the new "merchant Shipping Bill," and much more may be expected when an efficient and energetic staff of authorized persons is organized to carry its wise provisions into effect. The public press can also help materially by ventilating freely the circumstances of every wreck, and every questionable transaction on 'Change, of which it has any knowledge. We must seek to soothe the angry feeling of all sides, and we must seek to bring about a union in thonght and aim of the leaders of the mercantile interests. The great owners of the North must sacrifice some of their cherished notions, and the great owners of the South some of theirs; while the Board of Trade is strengthened by the united voice of the mercantile marine world, and not distracted by its opposed views and conflicting opinions.

In short, we know as well, and possibly better, than most other people, that the nation has good reason to be dissatisfied with the present state of the mercantile marine, and the numerous important interests connected therewith. And, moreover, having that great and holy cause of "saving life at sea" deeply at heart, we are desirous above all things that a great change for the better should take place therein, being firmly convinced that, however noble it may be to send help to the drowning mariner, however philanthropic to provide life-boats for the distressed ship, it is, to say the least, wiser to prevent the mariner from being unnecessarily exposed to danger: and more judicious to take measures to prevent, as far as possible, the vessel being wrecked at all. Holding these views, we also hold that every measure whensoever originated, which has for its object the improvement of the moral or social status of the sailor, the education of the officer, the greater sea-worthiness of the ship, and fairness and honesty of the monetary transactions connected therewith, is a measure directly, and very appreciably affecting the number of wrecks, and, as a necessary consequence, the number of lives lost at sea. We do not therefore desire to have the matter quashed, nor do we think "things are already at their best," but we deprecate ignorant criticism, and we appeal to the good sense of the public against wholesale abuse, and undeserved or unfair strictures.

In examining old papers I find the following circular and letters on the subject of lessening the dangers of navigating the Atlantic; all came from high authority, and while old navigators will say there is nothing new in them, I cannot but think the truths therein stated will be of use to some who do not profess to have learned everything in regard to their duty.

BOSTON, DEC. 25, 1854.

SIR,—In a preceding letter a reply was attempted to the important question, "*What can be done to lessen the risks of Ocean Navigation?*" In this connection a change of route to and from the North of Europe was recommended,—an extreme northerly course having for some years had the preference over a more direct one, and thereby ships have necessarily incurred the dangers of icebergs, of the fogs prevalent upon the Banks, and worse yet, of the rocks of Newfoundland. It was essayed to show that a course from the southern extremity of Ireland, Cape Clear, so shaped as to leave the southern point of Newfoundland, Cape Race, at least one hundred miles to the North, would materially lessen the dangers of the voyage. The only reason assigned for adherence to the Northern track is, that it shortens the passage. But the distance saved is vaguely estimated at from seventy-five miles to "a whole day's running distance," (three hundred miles,) a difference which certainly might seem to some sufficient to put the more prudent course out of the question. Who would not risk a thousand lives, rather than prolong the passage a day! Happily, this alternative is not presented, and caution and speed may be consulted in common, since, while approaching Cape Race no nearer than *one hundred miles*, the voyage from Europe will be increased only *twenty miles*. The verification of this fact is well worth all the attention which this discussion has received; that it rests upon more than mere assumption, will appear upon the authority of the subjoined letter from the learned and accurate Professor of Mathematics of Harvard University. His statement, much as it may surprise some navigators, will be valued in Europe as at home. I am also permitted to add the remarks of Messrs. C. H. Davis and M. F. Maury, distinguished as scientific officers of the United States Navy.

Another consideration not to be overlooked by the advocates for a northern course to shorten the passage is, that even the hour and a half apparently gained, may be greatly overbalanced by having to "run slow" through the region of fogs. The idea advanced, that any competent navigator, with scientific knowledge enough to entitle him to the command of an ocean steamer, would willingly run for a dangerous point merely to "sight it and verify his position," after a week at sea, is not to be entertained. There are truly perils enough to be dreaded in the ever shifting iceberg and scudding ships, particularly when shrouded in fog or night, to keep officers on the alert, without running purposely for rocks whose position is known.

THOMAS B. CURTIS.

Cambridge, Dec. 1, 1854.

My Dear Sir,—Permit me to thank you for your letter upon the propriety of giving Cape Race a clear berth in coming from England. It has induced me to make an exact computation of the gain in distance arising from the hazardous coasting of this point of land.

I find that for every mile by which the course of the voyage is removed from Cape Race at its nearest approach, the passage is prolonged one-fifth of a mile, or a minute in time, if the average speed of the ship is twelve miles an hour.

Sincerely and respectfully your friend,

T. B. Curtis, Esq. BENJAMIN PEIRCE.

National Observatory, Washington, Dec. 2, 1854.

Dear Sir,—I have this morning your favor, with a printed copy of your circular letter. I sympathize with you most heartily in your efforts to cause action in the right quarter, with the view of lessening the steam dangers of the sea. I wish, with all my heart, the owners of the lines and the insurance offices would take the matter up. I sent you all the charts I have which would be likely to be of any service to you.

Respectfully, &c.,

T. B. Curtis, Esq. M. F. MAURY.

Cambridge, Dec. 22, 1854.

My Dear Sir,—In connection with the views contained in your interesting letter of December 1, it may be satisfactory to you to know, that a vessel bound from St. George's Channel to New York, would only increase her distance twenty miles, if, instead of pursuing the great circle route to Cape Race, she were to take the great circle route to a point one hundred miles southeast of Cape Race, and go thence, by Mercator's sailing, to the light-boat off the shoals of Nantucket.

Very faithfully yours,

T. B. Curtis, Esq. C. H. DAVIS.

In the early part of my remarks, giving extracts from Manby's pamphlet of 1826, I find that I have not given him sufficient credit for his early and disinterested service in the cause of humanity.

In the Journal of the Life Boat Institution, for Jan. to Oct. 1855, is a memoir of Capt. Manby, from which it appears that he began his mortar experiments about 1783, and after much study and expense, with some help from the Board of Ordnance, he perfected his experiments; and on the 12th February, 1808, he rescued a crew of seven persons, from a wreck cast on shore in a N. E. gale. Previous to this successful trial in saving life, namely in 1792, Lieut. Bell, of the Royal Artillery had devised "a plan for throwing a line by means of a shell." Similar experiments were also made by a Frenchman named La Fere; Manby had never heard of these, he therefore is justly entitled to be considered the one who first successfully introduced throwing a line by a mortar to a wreck.

In 1810, after rescuing the crews of other vessels, he brought the mortar to the notice of Parliament and received substantial aid, and prior to 1824 had yielded his right in his apparatus to the Government; he died in December, 1854, aged 89.

Referring to what has been written in the foregoing pages, as to assistance to the Royal National Institution from the Government through the Board of Trade, I find by the *Life Boat Journal* of January 1870, which discusses the Merchants Shipping Act of 1869, that "in consequence of the noble manner in which the public have supported the Institution it has been enabled to relinquish pecuniary aid from the Board and thus successfully carry on its great work without any government help whatever."

The Mortar and Rocket apparatus is still managed by the Coast Guard, under the authority and at the expense of the Government.

A curious bit of history may here be recorded in regard to the establishment in 1853-4 of several life-boats on Sable Island. Miss D. L. Dix procured subscriptions for them from certain merchants and underwriters of New York, Philadelphia and Boston.

I have a letter before me, from Mr. Eben. Merriam, of Brooklyn, N. Y., who was at that time one of the leaders in all good works; he gives me under date January 8, 1855, quotation from a letter of Miss Dix, dated Liverpool, December 20, 1854; in which she quotes from a letter of the Honorable Hugh Bell, of Halifax, dated 7 December, the fact that the very day after the arrival at Sable Island of the boats, sent by Miss Dix, from New York; they rescued under very perilous circumstances, 180 persons from an American ship cast on shore about twenty miles from the Government station.

The boats are said to be Francis Metallic Life-boats. The Reliance and Grace Darling, 26 feet long, 7 feet wide; the Samaritan, 16 feet long; they were provided in the fall of 1853; were shipped for Halifax in a vessel that was wrecked on that coast, and as I understood at that time, the crew were saved by them.

They were damaged, returned to New York, repaired and shipped to Halifax, and as the rescue did not occur until late in '54, I presume they were long delayed repairing.

I had the pleasure of raising means in the fall of 1853 for one boat, built at Nantucket of wood, which was shipped on the 2nd December, 1853, by a Cunard steamer on account of Miss Dix, and which would have been shipped in the same vessel with the others but for what I wrote to her on the 27th October 1853 as follows:—"I think it would be best to send the New York and Philadelphia boats from New York, and the Boston boat from here, or to use a trite adage 'not put all your eggs in one basket.'"

The performance of the metallic boats was highly satisfactory on the occasion referred to.

It is to be hoped that the fact, of the placing four boats on an English Island by an American lady will not be forgotten.

Recent trials of the Francis metallic boats, received in 1855 from the Treasury Department, by the Humane Society of Massachusetts, proves that they are very hard to turn over by means of a parbuckle from a vessel, and that it requires about half of that power to turn them back again; this is owing principally to cork fenders lashed to the outside about eight inches below the gunwale. When turned bottom up several men can stand on them without making much impression, and when righted with the plugs out the water nearly comes up to the thwarts, or about nine inches below the gunwale.

Hence it will be seen that they are in no sense "life-boats," and as they pull heavy and are difficult to transport, they are quite useless, compared to light wooden boats for saving life. It is worthy of remark that in an experience of more than thirty years as a servant of the Humane Society, I do not call to mind but two or three cases of loss of life to the crews of the so-called life-boats, and one at least of these, was the result of running the boat before the sea, alongside of the wreck and suddenly checking her by the painter, when she slewed round, capsized, lost part of her crew, the rest floated safely to the beach.

In regard to charges for our 5½ inch mortars, recent trials show that 10 ounces of powder is about the maximum to insure the integrity of the line and becket; and in the small iron mortars, 4 ounces is about enough.

While writing my concluding lines I am shocked to learn of the loss by fire of the Missouri, near Abaco, on her way from New York to Havana, with news as yet, of only twelve or thirteen saved out of near an hundred souls.

It is safe to conclude that this large loss of life was principally owing to a want of preparation for the emergency, by due drill and organization.

Referring to what is said in the foregoing pages about the prize boat of the Royal National Institution and as to rockets and mortars, I give the result in a letter of Capt. J. R. Ward, who is the chief inspector and agent of the institution.

BURNHAM, SOMERSET, 25TH OCT. 1872.

My Dear Sir :

In answer to your questions :

1ST LIFE-BOATS :

As regards forms, the present life-boat of this Institution is somewhat sharper at the ends, but with a flatter floor than the boat of Mr. Beeching which gained the Northumberland prize. Its size, depth of keel, and its general form, varies according to local circumstances ; such as nature of the shore, number of men available to work it, whether likely to be cheifly used under sail or oars, etc.

As regards internal fittings, Beeching's boat was solely ballasted by a tank of water, and which being fitted on a wrong principal caused accidents attended with loss of life, which led to the discontinuance of water ballast altogether, in the self-righting boats.

The water in them was contained in a wide tank under the deck, covering about two-thirds the width of the boat, and as a consequence when only partially filled, which was liable to be the case, the water falling to the lee-side when under pressure of sail or struck by a sea it settled on that side like the shifted cargo of a loaded ship.

Had the ballast tanks been long and narrow and divided into compartments, the above danger would have been avoided, as whether full or only partially so, the water would have been confined to the central part of the boat, immediately over the keel.

This Institution however from the first adopted fixed ballast, consisting of a heavy cast iron keel and of a body of cork in water tight cases, or of solid fir wood beneath the deck. In consequence of its becoming decayed, the solid wood has for some years been given up, and the space under the deck is now filled with light water tight boxes (with air spaces between them for ventilation,) a certain number of these boxes in the central part of the boat being filled with cork. The weight of the keels varies in our 32 and 33 feet boats from 8 to 10 cwt., and of the boxes and cork under deck from 5 to 7 cwt. The manifold advantage of the system is that if a boat should be stove in the floor, the water space is so reduced below the deck, (the buoyancy of the empty and cork boxes then becoming available) that she could still take aboard a considerable number of persons besides her crew without being too deeply immersed.

2ND ROCKETS AND MORTARS:

This Institution gave up all connection with the supply and management of the Rocket and Mortar Apparatus as far back as 1854, since which time it has been exclusively in the hands of the Board of Trade, and with the exception of two or three local Volunteer Rocket Brigades is worked by the officers and men of the coast-guard.

The Board of Trade have still a certain number of Stations supplied with the Manby Mortar and shot, but on account of the greater portability and longer range of the Boxer *double* rocket, the latter is preferred and is mostly in use.

I am my dear sir,

Very faithfully yours,

J. R. WARD.

Just as I had determined to spread no more ink at this time on Life-boats, Anchor-shot, etc., I received the Life Boat Journal of November 1st,—No. 86, containing an elaborate article on boats for vessels of war, and another on anchor-shot for aiding the launch of the life-boats.

I have condensed the language so far as I could without impairing the sense and perhaps ought to apologize to the writers in advance for the liberty I take. I have already alluded to the Manby Grapnel Shot, p. 20, and the anchor of Capt. Jerningham, p. 24, as well as to Rodgers' anchor, pp. 28 to 32; but as my motive is to invite discussion and promote experiments for saving life, I shall rest content in the hope that my large sins of omission and commission will be forgiven *above* if not here below.

The article on anchor shot appears to have emanated from dissatisfaction on the part of Mr. J. B. Rodgers, because the Royal Institution according to his view, did not give encouragement to his apparatus; while I should like to see Rodgers' anchor fairly tried, I am inclined to think the inspectors of the Royal Institution, are right.

LIFE-BOATS FOR SHIPS OF WAR.

The melancholy accident which occurred to boats of H.M.S. *Ariadne*, in March last, has revived the questions as to the most suitable life-boats for ships, and the best apparatus for lowering them into the water.

A seaman had fallen overboard, the ship running ten knots, with the wind on the quarter. She was quickly hove to, and a cutter was sent in search of the man. The ship, dropping fast to leeward, steam was got up, and she was steered towards the boat; which was seen to broach to, and upset.

Another cutter was at once lowered, but one of the tackles fouling, she was swamped, with the loss of one man, the rest being with difficulty saved.

The ship was then placed in position as to drift toward the first boat, and, with very great difficulty, four of its crew were saved, two officers and eight seamen perished; besides the man who had fallen overboard, and both the boats were lost.

The *Ariadne* had no life-boat, the Admiralty having left it optional with the captains to have one or not.

The reasons for their not having them are:—

1st. That life-boats are heavier than ordinary boats.

2nd. Much of the space within them being occupied by the air compartments they have less space disposable for stowage.

3rd. That accidents to the boats of ships of war are unfrequent, therefore it is not worth while to sustain an inconvenience to meet a rare evil.

Before entering on the question of life-boats, we remark on the objections:

1st. Increased weight.

The increase need not be great, as the material of the air compartments can be of the lightest description consistent with strength. In a merchant vessel, this increase of weight, might be of consequence; but in a ship of war, it would not be worth consideration; and it would only be requisite to make the davits and fittings, and the hoisting gear stronger.

2nd. Stowage-room.

Undoubtedly a life-boat should not be used as a cargo boat, and there is little need for boats of a frigate to carry cargo, beyond armament and stores.

It is, however, most important that the stowage-room should not be diminished in the boats of a ship of war; a suitable life-boat has a positive advantage, since the air compartments forming its surplus buoyancy, form seats which is an advantage of a very important character.

3rd. Unfrequency of accidents to the boats of ships of war.

In time of peace accidents are not of frequent occurrence, but in time of war it would be often important to have at least one boat in every ship capable of going through a surf, or through a heavy sea, without serious risk to crew. The upsetting of a boat in attempting to cross the bar, off Kiel, in 1854-5, when Capt. JOHN FOOTE, R.N., was drowned, together with some of his men, may be quoted as an illustration of this need. Having reference, to times of peace, there are few ships which have cruised three years without having lost one or more men at sea, and we consider it a duty to every seaman that there should be means provided for his safety, in the event of his falling overboard; and that it is an equally imperative duty to provide the same for those who proceed to his aid.

It should not be optional with the captain to carry a life-boat or not, but every vessel should have one; and all the larger class should carry two, one on each side of the ship.

We regret that the Commission appointed by the Admiralty to enquire into the subject of boats and lowering apparatus, have reported that the boats supplied to ships of war are sufficient, and they consider also that the ordinary tackles used are all that is requisite.

We think that the Commission have forgotten the loss of Capt. FOOTE and his boat's crew; and that they did not sufficiently bear in mind the importance of being able to communicate safely at all times between the ships of a fleet and the shore.

On reading the evidence given before the Commission, we observe that whilst it is generally admitted that it would be an advantage to have a life-boat, they uniformly object to have one in lieu of an ordinary boat, but consider that there should be an extra one. They come to this conclusion from the belief that none of the present boats could be spared from the general use of the ship, whilst they say that a life-boat is unfitted for such use. It was also considered by some of them, that a cork belt outside, or more or less cork inside a boat, would be desirable.

We feel convinced that these difficulties may be easily met. There is, however, but one mode of giving a boat sufficient extra buoyancy to make her a life-boat, viz., by placing within her a large amount of enclosed air, in perfectly watertight cases, and by the distribution of the same in such a manner that it shall not only provide the requisite buoyancy, but greatly add to her stability and safety.

It was the opinion of the Commissioners and of the officers examined, that it is sufficient to make a boat insubmergible; we contend that no boat is worthy of the name of a life-boat, unless she floats high enough, after being filled by a sea, to be manageable; which a boat submerged to her thwarts, cannot be. Such a boat is, then, nothing more than a water life-buoy. In a moderate breeze, every sea would break into her, and she would be very crank. It is, therefore, an illusion to suppose that a little cork, either inside or outside, will make a life-boat. Some merchant vessels' thus fitted, are life-boats only in name. Cork, in the boats of the National Institution, is used as ballast; and it is too heavy for any other use.

Admitting, then, that enclosed air as being the lightest, is the only suitable one, the questions follow: what should be its amount, and how should it be distributed?

Its amount should be the greatest possible, without interfering with the use of the oars, and it should be distributed along the sides and the ends of a boat, where in the one case it will add to the lateral, and in the other to the longitudinal stability, for it follows that the buoyant or lifting property of the enclosed air on one side or at either end of a boat, when submerged, would powerfully tend to right her, whilst, if it is sufficient in amount, by confining the water within the boat to the centre, it acts as ballast, instead of rushing from side to side.

To effect this object the side cases should extend from floor to thwarts, conforming with the shape of the boat to the thwart level, and equal in width to one-fourth of the boat; the inner sides being perpendicular to check the rushing of the water from side to side with every motion of the boat. Also that the end cases should be each equal to one-eighth the length of the boat. These proportions have been tried, and found to give the qualities of extra buoyancy, stability, and steadiness.

It may be thought that so large an amount of enclosed air space at the sides would interfere with the free use of the oars and with stowage-room. It will be found, however, that in a double-banked boat, where the rowers sit close together, such is not the case, and the less will it be so if the upper inner angle of the side cases is cut off to allow depression of the oars to raise the blades above the sea. In a single-banked boat there would be more inconvenience, but we think all life-boats should, when practicable, be double-banked. Passengers can also be stowed more conveniently in such boats than in single-banked ones, as they can sit round the sides on the air-cases and thwarts without being in the way of the rowers.

As regards the stowage of cargo, the two functions are incompatible; but, if a ship's cutters are required to carry cargoes, other than human, in harbor, the side cases can be so fitted that they can be removed. This is the only way of meeting the difficulty. As to the amount of enclosed air-space, there can be no compromise, since in exact ratio to its increase is the water space decreased, and in the same ratio will the boat become manageable after being filled by a sea.

Another property in any life-boat worthy of the name, is self-relief of water to the outside level. Two holes of three inches diameter, fitted with plugs, would suffice to lower the water in the boat to the outside level, after shipping a heavy sea, when the remainder could be baled out.

Let the Admiralty cause a cutter, without any alteration in the model, (although such boats would be better sea-boats with round or pointed sterns,) to be fitted with portable air-cases, and then tested, when the advantages will be apparent.

In concluding these remarks, we cannot but express our regret that the Commissioners should have interrogated parties unconnected with this Institution as to the qualifications of its life-boats, which led to replies depreciatory of them, representing them as incapable of rowing to windward against a moderate wind; a defect which, if correct, would disqualify them for the work they are provided to do.

It is true that their success over a long period of years, and their very few failures to reach wrecked vessels, in the face of gales, entirely refutes such an opinion; yet no opportunity was afforded to bring forward evidence of the efficiency of its boats.

Anchor Shot as Aids to Launching Life-Boats.

In 1845 it was proposed to throw an anchor or grapnel from a mortar, with a line attached to it, to haul boats through a surf. A Mr. Offord, designed a grapnel with flukes or arms for that purpose, and in the following year Captain, now Admiral Jerningham, designed a folding anchor. Each weighed about 45 lbs., and was fired from Manby's brass 5½ inch mortars, with from 8 to 12 ounces of powder, carrying a 1½ inch Manilla line.

The anchor and grapnel were tried at Woolwich, in 1846, by the Royal Artillery, when a maximum range of 170 yards was attained. Capt. Jerningham's anchor had on a previous occasion ranged to 210 yards. Further trials were made on the coast in 1852, but it was considered that they had not sufficient holding power; that they could not be depended on for hauling a life-boat through a surf; and it is evident that if there should be any uncertainty at the moment of launching, such an instrument would be worse than useless: it would be like the broken bow in the hand of the hunter, or as the rotten staff in that of the pilgrim, which would fail them in the hour of need.

If any real want had been felt for such a contrivance, further experiments would have been made, and larger anchors from larger mortars have been tried; if no improvements had taken place in the life-boat carriage of that day, the want would have been felt; the requirement being to launch a life-boat without coming in contact with the ground, and with sufficient impetus to enable her to be got under command with oars or sails.

At an early period, the attention of the Institution was turned to the improvement of its life-boat carriages, and no pains or expense were spared to make them efficient, not only for transport, but as a means of launching a life-boat safely, quickly, and effectually. Those results were attained, and the carriage adopted answers every purpose. It has only to be drawn into the water by horses, or pushed into it by men, sufficiently far to insure the floating of the boat on leaving it, her bow being at the same time pointed at a right angle to the advancing waves, and her crew being seated in her with their oars in hand. She is then run with rapidity into the sea by means of self-detaching ropes, which are worked by people or horses on the shore, and is thus at once got under command. At the greater number of stations the shore is flat, and this plan is sufficient; but where a beach is steep a hauling-off rope is often an advantage.

At most of such localities a larger class of life-boat is stationed, which are unprovided with carriages, and at which places permanent warps are provided, attached to a buoy, moored at a sufficient distance from the shore. These warps are kept out through the winter months only.

Another mode of giving a boat this first impetus is by means of poles, called "sets," from 35 to 50 feet long, with an iron fork at one end, which being placed against the boat, and pushed by persons on the shore, are often very effective.

By these methods the life-boats of the Institution have been safely launched during the twenty years of their existence. The want of any further means to accompany boats by land on their carriages, has not been felt; and the Committee have not thought it necessary to experimentalize with a costly apparatus.

Nevertheless they have been called to account by inexperienced persons, many of whom have never even seen a life-boat launched to go to a wreck, for not adopting or making trial of a modification of the anchor and grapnel of Capt. Jerningham and Mr. Offord, as designed, a few years since, by a Mr. J. B. Rogers.

The distinction between their plan and his is, that theirs threw a single line, by which the crew had to haul themselves afloat; whereas his has a block attached to the anchor, and thereby carries a double line rove through the block, by which a larger line can be rove, and the boat be hauled off by persons on the shore.

Although throwing a small double line, with power to reeve a stouter one, is a great improvement on those which carried a single one, there would be serious inconveniences in its adoption; and the need of any such aid has not been sufficiently felt to induce the Committee to incur them. These inconveniences are:

1st. The apparatus and cart for its transport, and a house in which to keep it, would cost at least £150, which would be a serious expense to each life-boat.

2nd. It would require horse power to transport it to wrecks, whilst it is often difficult to procure enough to draw the life-boat on its carriage.

3rd. Delay would be occasioned both by the transport of the apparatus and the time occupied in loading and firing it, whilst it is questionable if the life-boat men would, in general, have patience to await the operation.

4th. As the life-boat men at nearly all stations are fishermen, pilots, or the owners of pleasure-boats, unaccustomed to the use of guns, and the services of Coast-guard men are rarely available, it has been thought that during the excitement which always prevails at such periods, and more especially in the night, accidents would be very likely to occur by its use.

5th. That at most stations, the shore being flat, the surf extends to several hundred yards from the shore; and all, therefore, that such an apparatus could do would be to haul a boat through the inner surf, and leave the greater surf to be encountered.

6th. Owing to the varying nature of the ground in different localities, and sometimes in the same locality, there would always be some uncertainty as to the anchor holding; the disadvantage of which defect we have already referred to.

But the want of such an apparatus has not been seriously felt; and surely those who are most interested in pursuing their work with success, whatever it may be, should be allowed to be the best judges of what they require.

The Life-Boat *Journal,* No. 86, contains a full account of the wrecks occurring on the coast of Great Britain in 1871, from which I derive the following facts:

The number of wrecks was 1,575, or 73 more than in 1870. The average loss,

1852–56,	1,045
1857–61,	1,320
1862–66,	1,611
1867–71,	1,575

Or an average of nearly 1,388 for the last 20 years. The least number was in 1853, being 832; and the largest in 1869, when 2,114 were lost. The loss of life during the last 11 years, from 1861 to 1871 inclusive, within a fraction of 800—the least number being 516, in 1864, and the greatest 1,333, in 1867. In the gale of October, 1859, when the Royal Charter was wrecked, 343 wrecks took place. In November, 1864, there were 264 wrecks; on the 2d of December, 1867, 146 were lost; on 22d and 23d August, 1868, more wrecks occurred than in any previous August.

Including the 1,575 wrecks with damages by collision, etc., there were casualties in 1871 amounting to 1,927, of which 1,668 were British, and of these 1,173 were coasters; and among the casualties were 351 by collision. The number reported as lost during ten years by reason of unseaworthiness is 524. Among the wrecks in 1871 were 506 colliers, many of them old and unsound; and in this year there were wrecked 155 nearly new, and 302 less than seven years old, 361 between 7 and 14, 554 between 15 and 30, 265 between 30 and 50, 44 between 50 and 60, 19 from 60 to 70, 6 from 70 to 80, 8 from 80 to 90, and 3 upwards of 100!—and the ages of 210 are unknown.

Of the wrecked and damaged in 1871—1,927—there were 223 steamers, 84 ships, 232 barks, 282 brigs, 219 brigantines, 493 schooners, 103 smacks, and the balance "small vessels of various rigs;" 806 were less than 100 tons, 687 from 100 to 300, 279 from 300 to 600, and only 155 *above* 600 *tons*. This fact speaks well for the better educated seamen of England. Of the 626 lives lost during 1871, 96 were lost in vessels foundering, 131 by collisions, 319 by being cast on shore, and 80 from various causes. During the year 4,336 were rescued by life-boats and other means. At the close of the year there were on the coasts of Great Britain 264 life-boats, of which 233 belonged to the Royal Institution and 31 to others; and there were 281 sets of rocket and mortar apparatus provided by the Board of Trade, under management of the coastguard. 129 "Volunteer Life Brigades" have been formed for instruction in the various methods in use for saving life and for co-operation with the coastguard.

It is worthy of note that nothing is said in these statistics relating to the proportion of loss in iron vessels as compared to wood. I take it for granted that most of the small craft were of wood, but it would be interesting to know the proportion of losses among the different classes in vessels at sea or on foreign shores.

It must be remembered that these statistics relate solely to the coasts of the United Kingdom.

It is to be hoped that the example in providing means to save life will be followed by this country, and that no efforts will be spared to induce Congress to appropriate means wherever local societies exist for the purpose.

Whether the means ought to be utilized under the prestige of the Government or by private associations, remains to be seen.

The British Merchant Shipping act and Navigation bill came into operation on the 1st of May, 1870.

It covers some three hundred long pages, and is arranged under eighteen heads, namely:

Part 1st, Covers 30 pages, and relates to registry, measurement, transfers, mortgages, character, liability of owners, forgery, evidence, etc.

2d, Covers over 70 pages, and relates to masters and seamen, mates, engineers, mercantile marine offices, apprentices, agreements, loss, wages, discharges, rights, seamen's savings banks, relief to families, leaving men abroad, volunteering for navy, provisions, health, accommodation, complaint, discipline, consular courts, registration of seamen.

3d, Covers 18 pages, and relates to collisions, equipments for safety, surveys of passenger steamers, order among passengers, accidents, carrying dangerous goods, cables and anchors.

4th, 4 pages, relates to delivery of goods on lien for freight exclusively.

5th, 8 pages, on general liability of owners.

6th, 22 pages, casualties, vessels in distress, wrecks, salvage of life and property, jurisdiction of courts, receivers of wrecks, fees of receivers, etc.

7th, 22 pages, pilotage, Trinity House, powers of authorities, returns, licenses, rights, dues, licensing masters and mates as pilots, offences, boats, pilot fund, etc.

8th, 14 pages, light-houses, sea-works, dues, authorities, construction, false lights and damages to light-houses.

9th, 14 pages, conservancy, inquiries, regulations as to works, obstructions to navigation, removal of shingle, etc.

10th, 14 pages, harbor dues, accounts, officers, regulations, warehouses, cranes, etc.,—life-boats, gauges, damage to harbor, battery sites, special and general acts.

11th, 3 pages, on loans to harbors.

12th, 2 pages, on powers by provisional orders.

13th, 5 pages, charges to shipping, liabilities, dues on ships sold, etc.

14th, 5 pages, Board of Trade, documents, forgeries, stamps, inspectors, etc.

15th, 5 pages, mercantile marine fund—its maintenance, uses, etc.

16th, 2 pages, on provisional orders.

17th, 14 pages, on legal proceedings, powers of judges, damages, punishment, etc.

18th, Miscellaneous, covering powers of commissioners, harbor-master, coasting trade, etc.

It would seem to be very wonderful if such a vast mass of red tape should work satisfactorily, yet it is believed that in no country in the world can the citizen on shore and at sea be said to be so carefully guarded as to his rights; and it may be said that if a redundancy of regulations for the protection of seamen be any evidence of their immunity from danger, they ought to feel quite safe.

In March last, Lieut.-Commander W. O'Neil of the Ohio made experiments, at my request, on the utility of the naval hammock as a life-preserver.

A cotton canvas hammock, with a mattress of cork shavings, sustained 160 lbs. of iron six minutes, 96 lbs. ten minutes, 62 lbs. one hour and five minutes, and 32 lbs. indefinitely. The same hammock and bed put into a close woven, cotton, canvas bag was floated *one hour and twelve minutes* against six minutes, *eight hours and a half* against ten minutes, and four hours against one hour and five minutes. It will be seen from this, that when the water gets through very slowly the buoyancy decreases, as a matter of course, but the hammock still floats nearly four times as long as without the bag. A further test showed that a common hammock and *hair bed* put into the bag floated twenty-four hours with one 32 lb. shot attached to it, and continued to float a long time, not stated, with two shots. Twenty hammocks thus provided will float an anchor weighing 2,000 lbs., and a hundred would float the largest anchor in the navy, or with a few spars and casks would make a raft to carry the crew of a frigate.

Sable Island Life-Boats.

Extract from report of Department of Marine and Fisheries, June 30, 1869:

"At Sable Island there is a staff of sixteen men maintained as a humane establishment, at a cost of upwards of $5,000 per annum; of this amount the British Government pay £400. A small sum is realized annually from the sale of cranberries grown on the island. Provisions for the staff are sent from the mainland."

Further extracts from the journal of the Assembly of Nova Scotia from 1865 to 1867, when the humane establishment was transferred to the Dominion of Canada:

"At Sable Island there have been three wrecks of small vessels, and one of a large American ship, the Acadia, from which 180 lives were saved, and in this case the safety of the passengers and crew is in a great measure to be attributed to the efficiency of the life-boats generously furnished by Miss Dix. The first shipment of boats were wrecked at Yarmouth, and replaced; the second shipment was driven into Yarmouth, and had only arrived a few days before the Acadia was wrecked; but for them few, if any, would have been saved."

Another report of H. Bell, C. B. W., of February 6, 1855, says:

"August 6, 1855, Sable Island was placed under the superintendence of R. S. Dodd. In 1856, two wrecks occurred, cargoes and crew saved; 1857, no wrecks; 1858, two wrecks, no particulars reported; 1859, no wrecks reported; 1860, brigantine Argo wrecked, crew and materials saved; 1861, no wrecks; 1862, May 7, ship Zone of Portland came on shore, one man lost,—August 1st, the Jane Lovett wrecked, crew saved; 1863, brig Gordon and steamer Georgia wrecked, crews saved; 1864, brigantine Dash, April 12, and schooner Weather Gage, 27th February, were lost, all saved,—March 8, schooner Langdon Gilmore of New York came on shore on the south side, captain and two men drowned, the remainder of the crew saved by the life-boat of the island—December 20th, brigantine William Bennett of St. Johns came on shore on the north side, crew all saved,—but two of the life-boat men, after the most brave and humane conduct, struggling in the surf during an inclement cold day to connect a line to the wreck, by which a female passenger and infant were safely landed, were exhausted by fatigue and cold, and perished on their way to their respective stations in the evening; 1865, brigantine Triumph of St. Johns was wrecked March 31, all hands saved,—ship Malakoff of Hull stranded June 12, on south side, crew saved. A large expenditure will be required to refit the life-boats which were damaged in the attempt to reach the W. Bennett, 1869. Bark M. and E. Robbins of Yarmouth wrecked February 24, on south side, two lives lost."

Although the above extracts are very meagre and indistinct as to the work done by the boats, they convey ample evidence of the value of the work done, principally through the active instrumentality of Miss Dix.

www.ingramcontent.com/pod-product-compliance
Lightning Source LLC
LaVergne TN
LVHW021358110826
845150LV00007B/1703

* 9 7 8 1 4 2 5 5 1 3 2 7 6 *